Reading in Content Areas

STRATEGIES FOR READING SUCCESS

Level D

Program Consultant
Dr. Kate Kinsella

San Francisco State University
San Francisco, California

Globe
Fearon

Upper Saddle River, New Jersey
www.globefearon.com

Consultants

John Edwin Cowen, Ed. D.
Assistant Professor, Education/Reading;
Program Coordinator, Graduate M.A.T./
Elementary Education
School of Education
Fairleigh Dickinson University
Teaneck, New Jersey

Dr. Kate Kinsella
Dept. of Secondary Education and
Step to College Program
San Francisco State University
San Francisco, California

Reviewers

Bettye J. Birden
Reading Specialist
McReynolds Middle School
Houston, TX

Sally Parker, M.A.
T.R. Smedberg Middle School/
Sheldon High School
Elk Grove, Unified School District
Elk Grove, CA

Georgeanne Herbeck
District Supervisor, Elementary Education
Perth Amboy, NJ

Kenneth J. Ratti
Science Department Chairman
Vaca Peña Middle School
Vacaville, CA

Senior Editor: Lynn W. Kloss
Editor: Monica Glina
Editorial Assistant: Kevin Iwano
Writers: Sandra Widener, Terri Flynn-Nason
Production Editor: Alan Dalgleish
Cover and Interior Design: Lisa Nuland
Electronic Page Production: José López
Manufacturing Buyer: Mark Cirillo

Photo Credits
p. 6: NBA Entertainment; p. 10: Wells Fargo Bank and Union Trust Company Historical Society; p. 15: F.A.S.E.;
p. 18: PhotoDisc, Inc.; p. 24: © Benjamin Mendlowitz; p. 28: Corbis/Bettmann-UPI; p. 32: Amazing Maize Maze;
p. 37: Corbis/Morton Beebe, S.F.; p. 50: Brown Brothers; p. 61: Corbis/Bettmann; p. 73: Allen Blake Sheldon,
Animals, Animals; p. 82: Corbis/David H. Wells; p. 85: Archive Photos; p. 105: Corbis/Bettmann;
p. 108: Courtesy of Kenneth Granderson.

Printed in the United States of America   5 6 7 8 9 10   03 02 01
ISBN: 0-835-95504-4

1-800-848-9500
www.globefearon.com

Contents

To the Student

The Hows and Whys of Reading

Think of a story that you've read. Maybe it was about someone's exciting adventure. What did you want to know about the story? What kinds of questions did you ask to get that information?

If you were reading an adventure story, you probably wanted to know *who* the characters were and *when* and *where* they were going. These questions are very helpful when reading *literary text,* which includes things like short stories, novels, plays, and myths. They all tell a story.

There is another kind of writing that is called *informational text.* This kind of writing informs the reader by giving opinions, explanations, reasons, facts, and examples about a certain topic. Things like chapters in a textbook and newspaper articles are considered informational text, so you are already familiar with this type of writing.

Good Questions for Literary Text	Good Questions for Informational Text
who	how
when	what
where	why

Think back to an example of literary text you've read. How are the questions you ask about a story different from the ones you ask when you read a chapter in your science book? In a science book, the questions *how*, *what*, and *why* are a great way to ask the "big" questions and get the information you are looking for. You might even start by changing the bold type headings and topic sentences into questions that begin with *how*, *what*, and *why*. Because *who, where,* and *when* can be answered with a simple fact or one-word answer, they are not as useful when reading informational text. Look at the following examples:

Heading		Question
Promoting Economic Growth	*becomes*	How can you promote economic growth?
Causes of Earthquakes	*becomes*	What causes earthquakes?
The Protests Affect U.S. Policy	*becomes*	Why do the protests affect U.S. policy?

These are examples of "big" questions. It is by asking these big questions that you will get the most out of the informational texts that you read. In this book, you'll learn more strategies for reading informational text and for remembering what you read.

Unit 1
Using Reading Strategies

When you plan a play in sports, you use a strategy. When you decide how to ask for something, you use a strategy. You probably already use a strategy when you read. When you pick up a book to read, you don't read just any book. You may look at the front and the back covers and quickly look through the inside. You have just used a reading strategy.

The reading strategies in this book will help you better understand what you read. You will be able to connect your reading to what you already know. Also, you will better remember what you read later.

The Benefits of Becoming an Active Reader

One goal of using reading strategies is to learn how to become an active reader. As an active reader, you respond to what you are reading with questions, ideas, and opinions. You also respond by taking notes on what you read. Finally, you think about what you read. What these steps have in common is that you are actively involved.

How Reading Strategies Work

You may find that one particular strategy always works well for you. You may find that different strategies work well for different kinds of reading. In every strategy, however, there are four basic steps. First, preview, or look quickly at what you will be reading. Second, read. Third, take notes. Fourth, review by writing a summary or thinking about your reading in another way. Below is a graphic of the steps you use with any reading strategy.

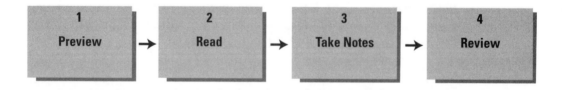

| 1 Preview | → | 2 Read | → | 3 Take Notes | → | 4 Review |

First, preview what you will be reading.
With any reading, your first step should be to think about what you are about to read. Previewing is the best way to do this. When you preview, you get an idea of what the reading will be about. You think about what you already know about the topic and get ready to learn new information.

Here are the steps to use when you preview:

1. Look at the title. Does it give you any clues about what you will read?

2. Look at the illustrations or diagrams and read the captions. Often, the main points in a reading are illustrated.

3. Read the first paragraph. The beginning of the article may include a summary of what is to come.

4. Read the last paragraph. The last paragraph may sum up the writer's main points.

Second, read carefully.
Reading carefully will help you understand what you are reading. If you find an unfamiliar word, check if the author has given you any context clues to help you figure out the word's meaning.

Third, take notes.
The kind of notes you take will vary depending on what you are reading. In math, your notes may be an explanation of how to solve a problem. In social studies, your notes may be a comparison of two countries. Taking notes is an active process. When you take notes, you have to put the information in your own words. This helps you remember the information.

Fourth, review your reading.
The kind of review you do may depend on the kind of reading you are doing and the strategy you choose. You may review a section in a math textbook by creating problems and solving them. You may review a science selection by making a diagram. Often, however, you will write a summary. To write a good summary, you must be able to remember what you read well enough to write a short paragraph that includes the main points of the reading.

How to Choose a Strategy

Different strategies work for different types of reading. Different strategies are needed because people learn and read in different ways. After trying different strategies, you may find that one seems to work best for you—you learn better when you use it. Try that strategy with different kinds of reading. You may have found the way that helps you learn best.

Strategy 1 KWL Plus

Understand It. . . . . . Active readers always approach reading with a strategy. They think about what they will be reading. They have an idea of why they are reading. After they read, they figure out whether they understand what they have read. KWL Plus (**K**now, **W**ant to Know, **L**earned) is one way of putting all those ideas to work for you. The "Plus" part on the strategy helps you put these pieces together by summarizing what you've learned.

Try It. . . . . The essay on pages 5–7 presents different opinions about the salaries of professional athletes. Follow along with a student who used the KWL Plus strategy.

The essay on pages 5–7

Step 1. Write what you already know about the topic.

When you think about what you already know, you focus your mind on what you will be reading. When you see new information, you will be able to connect it to what you know. After you think about the topic, preview the essay. Here's what the student thought as he considered the topic and then previewed the essay.

People on TV are always talking about the high salaries made by pro athletes. I remember reading something about how high Michael Jordan's salary was. This will probably be about whether players should be paid that much.

Look at what the student wrote in the K section of his KWL chart. Then add at least two things you know to the list.

K (What I know)	W (What I want to know)	L (What I've learned)
Some pro athletes earn high salaries.		

Step 2. Write what you want to know.

In the next section, you write questions that will help you focus your thinking as you read. Here is what the student thought:

I want to know what the arguments are for and against high salaries.

In the W section, the student listed two questions he wanted to answer. Add at least two things you want to learn as you read this selection.

K (What I know)	W (What I want to know)	L (What I've learned)
Some pro athletes earn high salaries.	Why are people against high salaries?	

Step 3. Write what you learn.

After you read the essay, write the important points in the L section of the KWL chart. Watch for information that answers your questions. You may learn important information that you did not ask questions about. Write notes about that information in the L column too. The student reading this article already wrote one main point that answers his first question.

K (What I know)	W (What I want to know)	L (What I've learned)
Some pro athletes earn high salaries.	Why are people against high salaries?	Against high salaries: Athletes aren't helping the world, so they don't deserve high salaries.

Strategy Tip

Thinking about why you are reading helps you focus your reading.

Strategy Tip

Notice that the section headings signal different opinions about the topic.

Debate: Are Pro Athletes' Salaries out of Control?

Should a basketball player earn more money for playing three minutes in a professional basketball game than a teacher makes in an entire year? Raise the topic of professional athletes' salaries in any group of people. Everyone has an opinion about this explosive issue. The following arguments include some, but certainly not all, of those opinions.

These Salaries Are Ridiculous!
It's easy to find people who get worked up about the kind of money athletes make. Statistics such as the one in the first paragraph horrify critics. Think about the kind of money athletes make compared to what most people earn. For example, during his top-earning pro basketball

years, Michael Jordan made $71,600 a night while he slept! Playing basketball does nothing to help the world. Basketball doesn't build houses for poor people or even feed them. Michael Jordan earned an absurd amount of money for playing a game!

Do you believe that professional athletes deserve their salaries?

Vocabulary Tip

Sometimes words you know are combined to make a phrase you might not know. If you look at the words *salary cap*, you'll see that the phrase is defined in the next part of the sentence.

Part of what makes NBA salaries absurd is the Larry Bird exception. Larry Bird was a very good NBA player. He negotiated an exception to the NBA's **salary cap**, which said that teams cannot spend more than $35 million a year for the salaries of all their players. The terms of this agreement changed in 1999. The 1999 agreement stated that players will be paid based on their number of years in the NBA. Players with 0–6 years of experience can make up to $9 million per year. Players with 7–9 years can earn up to $11 million per year. Those with 11 or more years can earn $14 million per year.

Out-of-control salaries have helped create the "big baby syndrome" among professional athletes. Many professional athletes are pampered and flattered and admired. They soon get the idea they are different from "ordinary" people. They don't have to play by the rules that the rest of us play by. They earn enormous amounts of money and can buy their way out of trouble. Some professional athletes never grow up. They don't have to because they can pay someone else to handle their responsibilities.

Professional athletes make poor role models. Younger athletes look at the lives the pros lead and want to be like them. "If those guys can make so much money playing ball," young athletes reason, "so can I!" As a result, thousands of young men neglect their education. Dreams of immense wealth lead young people to base their future on unrealistic expectations. They often find themselves unprepared to do anything when they fail to make the cut.

What kind of message do sky-high salaries for athletes send about what is important? The comparison between a teacher's pay and a professional athlete's might be obvious. It's also accurate. What does that tell us about our society? What should we conclude when people who contribute to society can barely feed their families, but those who handle a ball well are millionaires?

Professional Players Are Worth What They Get

Plenty of people believe that professional athletes deserve every penny they get. Who else, they argue, provides so much entertainment

to others? A great team can make a community proud, and that's worth just about any amount of money.

Why don't people who do worthy work earn as much money as professional athletes? That's simple. Those people don't create as much **revenue** for their employers. Athletes create enormous amounts of revenue, so the owners can justify the players' salaries. Should all that money go right into the pockets of the owners? Of course not! It should go to the players, who provide what people pay to watch.

Athletes, of course, understand the way our world works. People often judge a person's worth by the money he or she makes. Athletes want big money not just for its own sake but also for the sense of self-worth it gives them. The size of the salary shows what an athlete is worth compared to other players.

Professional athletes' salaries reflect our economic system. Our country has **prospered** because it is a free-market system. People who provide something the market wants can charge whatever people will pay for it. If something costs $50 million and someone will pay that price, that's what the "something" is worth. That's what happens in a free market. That's the American way—the way that has given us an economy and a society that have flourished. There is no reason to condemn those who have done nothing more than make the system work for them.

Vocabulary Tip

Look for clues for the meaning of *revenue* in this paragraph. Athletes create enormous amounts of it. What does *revenue* mean?

Vocabulary Tip

You may know that the word *prospered* means "to have benefited." In this sentence, *prospered* means our country has benefited from a free-market system.

4. Use the KWL chart to summarize what you have learned.

When you write a summary, you make a quick check of what you read. Do the main points stay with you? Can you point to the important arguments in what you read?

Here's how the student began his summary. Use this beginning as a model to write your own summary on another sheet of paper.

This essay states the arguments for and against high salaries for professional athletes . . .

Apply It. . . . . Try the KWL Plus strategy on a reading assignment you have. First, draw a KWL chart on another sheet of paper. Identify the topic and then fill in the K section with what you already know about it. Preview the reading, then fill in the W section with what you want to learn from your reading. After you read, fill in the L section. Then use your completed KWL chart to help you write a summary of your reading.

Strategy 2 Cornell Note-taking

Understand It...... The Cornell Note-taking strategy works well for taking notes after you read. You review the important points of the selection. Then you find support for each point. If you understand the main points, you understand the reading. Focusing on the details that support the main points will help you remember more about what the author is telling you.

When you take notes after you read, you do more than just write down whatever you see. Your notes should focus on the main points, not the minor ones. Generally, you won't copy the author's exact words. Instead, you will rewrite the author's ideas in your own words. When you finish, you should have a good idea of what you just read.

Try It.............. The article on pages 9–11 is about women who made the difficult journey to the Yukon Territory during the gold rush in the 1880s and early 1900s. Follow along with a student who read the article and took notes using the Cornell strategy.

Strategy Tip

Before you read, think about *why* you are reading. What do you need to find out?

Step 1. Preview what you will read.

Before you read, you need to preview the material. If you are looking at a textbook for the first time, preview the table of contents. Then look quickly at the selection you will read. Look at the title and subheadings. Also, read the first and last paragraphs and topic sentences. See what the author is telling you. As you preview, jot down some questions about what interests you about the reading. Below are some of the questions the student had after she previewed. Add your own questions to the list.

When was the gold rush?

How did women survive the harsh weather in the Yukon?

Why did they go?

_____

_____

_____

Strategy Tip

Leave space between main ideas so you have enough space in the Evidence/Details column to write supporting evidence.

Step 2. Read, and then take notes.

When you take notes using the Cornell system, you divide a piece of paper into two sections. In the Main Points column, you list key words and ideas. In the Evidence/Details column, you list details that explain each idea or evidence that supports the idea.

Here is how the student began her note-taking on the article on pages 9–11. Add your own notes to her list.

Main Points	Evidence/Details
The Yukon was seen as a man's world. Some women went north, too.	Men went north to earn money. Women went north for many of the same reasons as men.

When Women Rushed for Gold

In the late 1800s, the United States was in an economic depression. People lost their jobs and went hungry. When the cry of "gold!" came from the Far North, many needed little urging to pack up what they did have and head north. This movement became known as the "gold rush."

The Yukon was seen as a man's world. Although the westward journeys of the pioneers were difficult, many families made new beginnings. The rush north was different. Travelers often had to carry everything they had on their backs. They had to cross raging streams and travel through treacherous mountain passes. They suffered through extremely cold winters and lived through times when they had little to eat. Women were generally considered neither as strong nor as resourceful as men. The view at the time was that women needed to be protected from the harshness of life.

Even so, about one of every ten people who made the difficult trip to Alaska and the Yukon was a woman. Women went for many of the same reasons men went—to find gold, to make a fortune, to find adventure. Some professional women wrote for newspapers, taught, or sold insurance. Any woman who could make a homesick miner a good meal or do his laundry could make plenty of money. Many women also went north with husbands who hoped to strike it rich. They came from all over the world. They helped write the history of a land filled with hardship, wealth, hope, and struggle.

A Mother's Search Leads to Employment

In 1894, Anna DeGraf set out for the Yukon. She was searching for her son, who had followed the lure of gold. The 55-year-old woman traveled across Chilkoot Pass in early spring. With her feet wrapped in rags, she walked with the aid of a crutch. "We had to climb over and around jagged rocks, sometimes jumping from one to another like mountain goats," she wrote in her diary.

DeGraf took her sewing machine so that she would be able to make her living while she looked for her son. She journeyed 800 miles down the Yukon River, asking about her son at settlements along the way. She made clothing for the miners and sewed tents. When she finally decided to give up and go back home, she sold her sewing machine and took her earnings home. She had $1,200 in gold dust. During the next 20 years, she traveled repeatedly to the North, searching for her son. She died at the age of 91 in San Francisco without ever finding him.

A group of four miners—three men and one woman—panning for gold

Golden Opportunity for Women

Some women went north to look for gold themselves. In 1874, Nellie Cashman began prospecting for gold. Prospecting was difficult for a woman. Some men refused to follow a woman's orders. Cashman, though, never seemed bothered by the attitudes she found and continued prospecting for gold. By winter of that year, she had returned to British Columbia. When she heard stories of prospectors trapped farther north in the gold fields, starving in the brutal weather, she organized a rescue party and led it back into the mountains. The food the rescuers carried saved the miners' lives.

Many women saw opportunities to make a living serving the needs of the miners. Harriet Pullen went north to Skagway, Alaska, in 1897. She didn't know anyone—but she did know that she would find opportunities to make money. Pullen found work as a cook and soon realized that many miners missed the taste of home. She used dried apples to make pies, which the miners **coveted**. Realizing that she could make money transporting the miners and their supplies, Pullen started a company. She became wealthy and began converting one of the grandest private homes in Skagway into the Pullen House, one of Alaska's finest hotels.

Native Americans

Some Native American women who grew up in the Far North got caught up in the gold rush as miners and hangers-on swarmed over the land where gold had been discovered. One woman, named Sinrock Mary, was the daughter of a Russian trader and an Inupiat woman. After her husband died, she won the right to own half of the couple's 500 reindeer. Miners were desperate for her reindeer, both for transportation and for food.

Vocabulary Tip

Look at clues in the paragraph to figure out the meaning of *coveted*. How did the miners feel about Pullen's pies?

In 1900, a group of miners followed her. They shot at her herd to scatter it and even offered her marriage and money. She refused and kept the herd together. When she sold her animals for meat, it was on her terms. She became the richest Native American woman in the North. Sinrock Mary adopted several children, who became reindeer herders themselves. Then she married another Inupiat man. She was known among her people for being smart, as well as generous with her time and money.

The women of the Yukon braved terrible conditions and sometimes loneliness and heartache to build lives for themselves in a difficult land. The women who went north with the gold rush did what they could to survive and prosper.

Step 3. Summarize what you have read.

Strategy Tip

Before you begin your summary, review your notes. Underline or highlight important words or phrases. That will help you remember them.

Look at the questions you asked in Step 1. Did you find the answers in the article? If you didn't, look over the article again. When you think you have all the information you need, write a summary of the article. The summary should include all the important points in the article and information that backs them up. Here is the way the student began her summary.

Summary

Although the Yukon was seen as a man's world, some women went north, too. They went to find gold and new adventures.

Now write your own summary: _____

_____

_____

_____

Step 4. Review what you have learned.

Did you learn what was in the article? Fold your Cornell chart so that only the left side shows. Can you remember the details and supporting evidence you wrote? If you can't, you may need to read the article again.

Apply It . . . . Try the Cornell Note-taking strategy on a reading assignment you have. Make sure you ask questions as you preview. Divide your paper as you take notes on the main points and write a summary to help you review what you have learned.

Strategy 3 PLAN

Understand It...... The PLAN strategy works well for people who learn best when they can make a picture of what they are learning. PLAN stands for **P**redict, **L**ocate, **A**dd, and **N**ote. When you use PLAN, you use words to build a word map that helps you understand what you will read.

There are many ways to draw word maps. If all the information in a reading relates to one subject, you might draw a wheel-and-spoke diagram. Write the subject in the center circle and the supporting details in the circles around it.

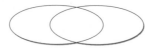

If an article compares and contrasts two different things, a Venn diagram might work best. Write the ideas that the subjects have in common in the space that links both circles. Write the information that is true of only one subject in one of the outer circles.

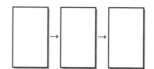

If an article is organized by time, you can create a sequence chart with arrows leading from one event to another.

Maybe you know another way to show how a piece of writing is organized. Feel free to use any kind of drawing, or graphic, that helps you organize the information you're learning.

Try It.............. Once you choose a graphic, locate and add information to it from your reading that tells you whether your ideas were right. Then fill in the word map with that information. Finally, note your understanding of what you read.

The article on pages 14–15 profiles Jaime Escalante, a teacher whose life and work inspired the movie *Stand and Deliver*. A student used PLAN as he read to help him understand the article. Read along to learn the PLAN strategy.

Step 1. Predict what you will learn.

When the student previewed the article, he didn't see any subheadings. After thinking about what he noticed as he previewed, he began a sequence chart. This is what he thought:

By previewing and by looking at the dates, I can tell that the article is arranged in time order. I think I'll try a sequence chart that shows major events in Escalante's life arranged in order.

Continue the sequence chart the student began. Preview the selection and make your predictions about what you think will be in the article. Write one prediction for each major event in each box. You may add more boxes. This is what the student wrote in the first box:

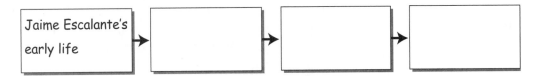

Step 2. Locate important information as you preview.

Look at the sequence chart. Put a check mark next to ideas or people you know something about. Put a question mark next to those you do not know. This will help you think about what you already know about the subject and prepare you to better understand what you read. This is what the student thought as he decided how to continue his sequence chart:

I don't know much about Escalante. I'll put a question mark in this box.

The student's word map looked like this:

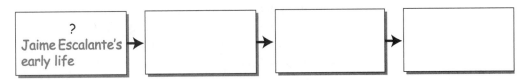

Step 3. Add information to your sequence chart.

Now read the selection. After you read, add information to your word map. Write in words or short phrases that remind you of the supporting facts or details under each main point. If you missed main points, add them to the map along with details that support the points.

Fill in the sequence chart after you read. Add major events in Escalante's life and write words that will remind you of evidence or details for each point. Here's how the student continued filling in his word map:

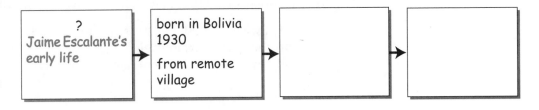

To Stand and Deliver

Jaime Escalante was born in La Paz, Bolivia, in 1930. His parents taught school in Achacachi, a tiny Indian village. When he was nine, his mother left his father and took the children to live in La Paz.

When he grew to adulthood, Escalante became a teacher in Bolivia and earned a reputation for his entertaining style and his success with students. In 1963, Escalante moved to the United States with his wife and son. The **political uncertainty** in Bolivia and the very low salaries for teachers convinced him it was time to leave.

Once in the United States, Escalante got a job washing dishes. No problem, he told his wife, Fabiola. He would learn English, send in his teaching credentials, and get a job as a teacher. The state of California disagreed. He would have to repeat college and spend another year getting a Master's degree before he could teach. Escalante was shocked. All his years of teaching and all his awards meant nothing.

Escalante followed the advice he had written on wall posters wherever he had taught: DETERMINATION + HARD WORK + DISCIPLINE = SUCCESS. For seven long years, he worked during the day and went to school at night. At times, Escalante became discouraged, but he kept going. Finally, he succeeded and got his teaching license.

Then, some would say, the hard part began. When Escalante walked into his first class at Garfield High School in East Los Angeles, he was distressed. He saw a group of angry teenagers who didn't want to be there, and who saw no reason to learn math. The school seemed to be run by gangs. Most of the teachers seemed to have given up.

Escalante didn't give up. He tried every possible way to reach his students. Bit by bit, he became known for his sense of fun and tough standards. However, no one in the school was prepared for his announcement in 1978. He planned to teach an Advanced Placement (AP) calculus class. Only 2% of high school seniors in the country take the difficult test. Those who pass earn college credit. Few Garfield students took any AP tests. No one thought Escalante would be able to turn his students into calculus scholars. Only five students made it through the class that first year. Of the five, only one passed the test.

Another teacher might have given up. Escalante just doubled his efforts. In 1979, nine students signed up, and six passed the test. In 1980, 15 students took the class, and 14 passed the AP test.

In 1981, Escalante had 18 students in his AP class. They worked harder than they ever had in their lives. They arrived at 7 A.M., stayed after school, and attended school Saturday mornings. One day during

Vocabulary Tip

What might *political uncertainty* be? You know that *politics* relates to government. You also know that uncertain means "not certain" or "not sure." So you can guess that *political uncertainty* means that the government might not last.

Strategy Tip

Notice that this biography has a lot of dates. Use them to create your sequence chart.

that year, Escalante left class after feeling a sharp pain. He passed out and woke up in a hospital. Escalante brushed aside the concerned doctors and went back to school. This only made his legend at Garfield grow.

Jaime Escalante

The hard work paid off. Every one of the 18 students passed the AP calculus test. The achievement was remarkable for any school but almost unbelievable for a troubled school like Garfield. The testing service that sponsored the test accused the students of cheating! Escalante was furious but finally agreed to let 12 of the students take the test again. Every one of them passed again. The story drew the interest of Hollywood producers. The movie *Stand and Deliver* was based on Escalante's work at Garfield High. Jaime Escalante became one of the most celebrated teachers in the United States.

Escalante was recognized as a "national treasure" by President Ronald Reagan. Escalante now teaches in Sacramento, California. He wants to show that his success can be repeated. According to Escalante, "When hard work is combined with love, humor, and a recognition of the desire to learn, the stereotypes and the barriers begin to crumble."

Strategy Tip

Using different-colored highlighters can help you remember what you read. Highlight the main point in one color and the supporting details in another color.

Step 4. Note what you have learned.

In this step, you note what you learned by reviewing it. You might close your eyes and review the important points or write a summary. You might redraw your word map. The note-taking step is important. It helps you remember what you read.

You can use the word map you made to help study. The notes you made will also help you review for tests.

Apply It. . . . . Use the PLAN strategy with a reading assignment you have. Preview the reading to decide how it is organized. Next, draw a word map of the main points and make check marks to note what you know. Put question marks next to things you don't know. After you read, write main ideas you did not already write and the ideas that support each main idea. Finally, note and review your work by writing a summary or using another way to make sure you will remember what you read.

Strategy 4 DRTA

Understand It...... DRTA stands for **D**irected **R**eading and **T**hinking **A**ctivity. The DRTA strategy works well when you can make some predictions about what you will read.

When you use DRTA, you focus on what the author is telling you by previewing the topic sentences, subheadings, illustrations, and charts. You make predictions about what an article will be about, read to see if your ideas are correct, and change your predictions if necessary. You make sure you understand the evidence that supports the main point of the writing.

When you use DRTA, you become an active reader. You look at the writing with an idea in mind—checking your predictions. When you finish, you make sure you understand what you have read.

Try It.............. The reading on pages 17–19 is about the hot dog and its place in U.S. society. You probably know something about hot dogs. Follow along with a student who used the DRTA strategy as she read.

Step 1. Preview to predict what you will read.

When the student first previewed the selection, she looked at the title, the subheadings, and the illustration. This is what she thought:

This article is about the history of the hot dog and how important it is in America today.

Based on what she saw, she made a couple of predictions about what she would learn. She wrote them in the first box of the DRTA graphic. Preview the selection and add your predictions to those the student made.

Strategy Tip
The student's second prediction is based on the first subheading. That often works, but not always. You need to preview the article to see whether the subheading describes the rest of the section.

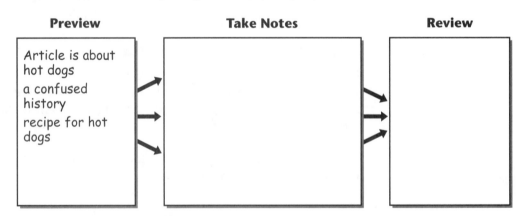

Preview	Take Notes	Review
Article is about hot dogs a confused history recipe for hot dogs		

Step 2. Read, and then take notes.

Read the selection. Then look back for evidence that supports your predictions. Write it in the Take Notes box. If your predictions were wrong, cross them off. Write facts about what you did read and evidence to support them. Here's how the student began reading and thinking about the predictions she made:

I was right. This is about the hot dog. The first part is about the hot dog's history.

After you read, look at the predictions you made. Find evidence that supports them and list it as this student did. Notice the evidence the student wrote:

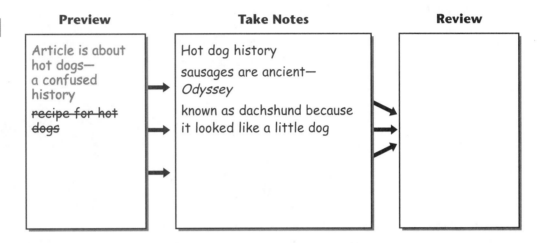

Preview

Article is about hot dogs—
a confused history

~~recipe for hot dogs~~

Take Notes

Hot dog history

sausages are ancient—
Odyssey

known as dachshund because it looked like a little dog

Review

Hot Dog! The Whole Meaty Story

Our story begins way back in the 9th century B.C.—or it may begin with Charles Felman, a German butcher who sold sausages in Coney Island, New York, in 1871. Then again, the glorious story of the hot dog may begin with an unknown German immigrant who had a push cart in New York City in the 1860s. The truth is, the name of the inventor of this beloved food is as mysterious as the inside of the hot dog itself. Over the years, though, the fame of this once-humble sandwich has grown. The hot dog has eaten its way into the heart of American culture.

The Confused Origins of the Beloved Dog

Sausages, those mixtures of ground-up meat and spices, are an ancient food. There is even a reference to a sausage in the Greek epic *The Odyssey*. The hot dog was first known as a dachshund (a species of dog that is long and low to the ground), or "little dog," because of the way it looked. The dachshund sausage is often credited to Frankfurt, Germany, in the 1500s. Some people, though, are sure the hot dog (also called the frankfurter) was invented in the late 1600s by a German butcher named Johann Georghehner. When he went to Frankfurt to sell his creation, the name *frankfurter* stuck. Then again, in Vienna, which is called Wien in Austria, the people are convinced the hot dog—the wiener—was born in their Austrian city.

Although it first appeared in Europe, the hot dog traveled to the United States in the late 1800s. Many have claimed that they were the first to serve the small sausages in America. One report says that a

German butcher named Charles Feltman sold 3,684 dachshund sausages in 1871 at Coney Island, an amusement park in New York.

The hot dog bun may date to 1904 in St. Louis. A **vendor** there was selling the hot sausages and lending his customers white gloves to use while they ate them. The gloves rarely came back. The vendor asked his brother-in-law, a baker, to make him some rolls to fit the meat. The hot dog bun was born.

Vocabulary Tip

If you don't know the meaning of the word *vendor*, think about related words you might know, such as *vending machine.* You know that vending machines sell things. The suffix *-or* often means "one who does something." So, a *vendor* is someone who sells things.

The name "hot dog" dates from 1901, when a man named Harry Stevens was trying to get a New York City Giants baseball crowd to buy food. Few people were buying the sodas, ice cream, and hard-boiled eggs Stevens's vendors were selling. Stevens sent men out to butcher stores to buy some small sausages—dachshund sausages. Stevens filled tanks with hot water and dumped in the sausages for his vendors to sell. "Get your red-hot dachshund sausages!" they cried. People loved them.

All-American hot dog stand

Tradition has it that a bored sports cartoonist named Tad Dorgan drew a cartoon of a barking dachshund settled into a roll when he saw Stevens's vendors that day. Not knowing how to spell *dachshund*, he wrote "hot dog" on the cartoon.

The sandwiches were a hit, but Dorgan's name for them stuck too well. Some people thought the nickname described the ingredients in the sausage. Rumors of dog meat in the sausages became known to most of the hot-dog-eating public. The Coney Island Chamber of Commerce, which governed the amusement park, passed a rule that sellers of hot dogs couldn't call them "hot dogs." They could call them "Coney Islands," or "red hots," or "wieners"—anything but "hot dogs."

Strategy Tip

What details can you add to your DRTA chart to explain the hot dog's confused history?

Hot Dogs Today

These days, no one seriously thinks that hot dogs contain dog meat. The sausages are more popular than ever. Americans eat about 20 billion hot dogs every year, which equals about 60 hot dogs for every American. Just in ballparks, people eat 26 million hot dogs. That's about four hot dogs for every 10 tickets sold.

Occasionally, activists try to scare the hot dog-eating public with tales of the ingredients that go into hot dogs. In 1972, the consumer

activist Ralph Nader called the hot dog a "deadly pink missile" because of the chemicals it contains. Vegetarians, who believe that people should not eat meat of any sort, routinely protest at hot-dog-eating contests. So what is inside those tubes? Mostly, it is pork and beef, although some hot dogs are made of chicken and turkey. They also contain water, salt, sugar, spices, and chemicals to cure the meat. Up to 3.5 percent of a hot dog can contain ingredients such as nonfat milk or grains.

The hot dog has traveled beyond its humble beginnings. Today there is a hot dog hall of fame, a newspaper called *The Frankfurter Chronicles*, and claims from different regions of the country that only they know how to make and eat a hot dog. New Yorkers like their dogs spicy. In St. Louis, Missouri, hot-dog eaters like their dogs cooked on a griddle. In Milwaukee, Wisconsin, people love bratwurst, another type of sausage, more than the hot dog. In the Southwest, a hot dog with a spicy Mexican taste is popular. Texans like corn dogs best.

While the hot dog is American, it has deep roots in Europe and is exported around the world. The hot dog is just too good to keep as an American secret.

Step 3. Review what you have learned.

Strategy Tip

When you summarize the article, be sure to include details about the creation of hot dogs and about their popularity today.

After you read, make sure that you not only understand what you read but also remember it. Can you close your eyes and think of the main points? Here's what the student thought about her review:

I think I understand the main points. The article is about the history of the hot dog and about how people eat them today.

Check your understanding. Write a summary in the Review box on page 17. A clear summary that includes the important points of what you read can help you remember your reading.

Apply It. . . . . Use the DRTA strategy with a reading assignment you have. Preview what you will read. Look at the title, subheadings, photos, illustrations, and topic sentences. Write predictions about what the selection will focus on. When you read, check to see if your predictions are right. Write facts and supporting evidence for the points you predicted. If you missed any major points, write them and the evidence that supports or explains them. Finally, write a summary to help you remember the information.

The predictions and notes you took will be helpful for studying later on. If you took good notes and organized your ideas logically in a summary, those notes should be all you need to review before you take a test.

Unit 2
Reading in Language Arts

When you think of language arts reading, you may think of grammar textbooks. Language arts is much more, though. It includes diaries, adventure tales, and magazine articles. Fun reading, such as short stories or mystery novels, is also language arts reading.

How Language Arts Reading Is Organized

Language arts has many kinds of readings, but there are only a few ways to organize these readings. Previewing will tell you which pattern the writer has chosen. If you can recognize the pattern, you will be able to predict better what is coming next as you read. Here are a few of the common patterns you will see in language arts reading.

Main Idea and Details. This is probably the most common pattern you will see in language arts reading. In this pattern, everything in the reading is connected to the main idea. In a textbook, the topic may be how to read poetry. In a magazine article, you may be reading about an invention. Once you recognize this pattern, you know what to look for: one or more main points, with each main point supported by important details or evidence. Here is an example of the main idea and supporting details pattern:

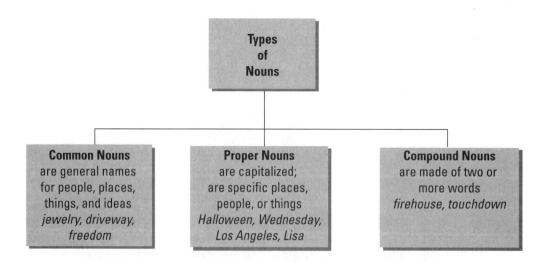

Compare and Contrast. With this pattern, the writer compares two or more things, such as types of poetry or periods in literature. When you see this pattern, consider making a Venn diagram like the one on the next page to help you understand the points the author is making.

Comparing Two Performances of Shakespeare's *Macbeth*

Gordon High School
staging poor
scenery boring

Both
strong actors playing Macbeth
lighting good

Dream Players
supporting characters weak
scenery great

Sequence of Events. When you see a series of dates or entries, you can guess that the events occur over a period of time. Examples of this are journals and diaries. True-life adventure stories and biographies may be written in time order. You may also see this pattern in fiction that moves forward in time. When you see a sequence of events, make your own sequence chart like the one below. That will help you remember the major events and when they occur in the reading.

A Suffragette is Born

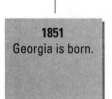

| **1851** Georgia is born. | **1869** She marries Frank. | **1870** They move to Nebraska. | **1872** Child, Brian, is born. | **1880** Georgia becomes a suffragette. |

Getting the Most from Your Reading

Once you can recognize patterns in reading, you will better understand what you read. You will think about what kind of information might be next. You also will better understand how all the points in the reading fit together. Thinking about how text is organized can help you become a more active reader.

Lesson 1

True Adventure: Adrift!

Understand It . . . . . .

Hint
You can review the Cornell Note-taking strategy on page 8.

This true story describes the journey of Steven Callahan, who survived 76 days in a rubber raft on the ocean. Since you may not know about the difficulties of life in a raft, try using the Cornell Note-taking strategy with the story. With this strategy, you take notes about what you've read.

Try It . . . .

First, preview the selection to get an idea of what you will read. Then divide a sheet of paper as shown in the Cornell chart below. Read the selection, then take notes. In the Main Points column, write the major points. In the Evidence/Details column, write the details and supporting evidence that explain each main point. After you're finished, you will write a summary of the selection.

Strategy Tip
As you write main points in the Main Points column, make sure to leave enough room for supporting information in the Evidence/Details column.

Main Points	Evidence/Details

Strategy Tip
Consider using a pencil instead of a pen when you take notes. It's much easier to revise your work.

Adrift!

Please don't go, Steven Callahan thought desperately. *Don't go down. Not yet.* It was no use. The sea rose up, up, up, and seemed to stay there forever. Then the waves crashed. Callahan looked on helplessly from his five-and-a-half foot rubber raft as his sailboat sank.

Callahan found himself 450 miles from land with only the few supplies he had been able to drag aboard the raft before his sailboat, the *Napoleon Solo,* finally went down. What Callahan didn't know was that he was about to set a record for surviving in a rubber raft for 76 days.

During the first days, Callahan lived on hope. His emergency radio beacon had a range of 250 miles. Unfortunately, he was 800 miles from the Canary Islands, 450 from the Cape Verde Islands, and 450 miles east of the nearest shipping lanes. *Should I turn on the radio?* he thought. *Who am I kidding? There's no one to hear me.*

There was an emergency bag on the raft. Callahan had six pints of water, two paddles, and two solar stills that could turn moisture from the air into drinkable water. He had a first-aid kit, a flashlight, a raft-patching kit, 50 feet of twine and a hook to use for fishing, and a speargun. Callahan had a few other assorted tools and a bit of food: 10 ounces of peanuts, 16 ounces of baked beans, 10 ounces of corned beef, and 10 ounces of raisins. It was not enough, but it was all he had.

The emergency kit also had a pencil and paper. From his first day on the raft, Callahan kept detailed notes about his position, his mood, and how he was surviving. Those notes later became the basis for his best-selling book, *Adrift*. Callahan felt desperate. He wanted to cry but told himself he couldn't afford to lose water through tears. It was February 6, only his second day on the raft.

Hunger Sets In

Callahan had some immediate concerns. He had to get the solar still working. He could last only a few days with the water he had. He rationed himself to a mouthful every six hours or so, drinking only half a pint of water a day. It was torture. The first solar still didn't work at all. The second collected eight ounces of water in an hour, and Callahan's spirits rose—until he tasted the water and tasted salt. He sat in despair until he saw a fin slice through the water. Suddenly, Callahan was alert. He didn't think *shark*; he saw food. He clawed through his bag to find his speargun, aimed, and took a shot. He missed. The shark swam back deep underwater.

He was always hungry. The little food he had was gone. The water situation was even more critical. Callahan ripped apart one still and used it to fix the other. He watched with delight as pure water dripped into the bag.

Finally, Callahan had hope. He had water. He could live at least 20 more days, even if he never found a way to catch fish or find food. Now, Callahan's major problem was sharks. He feared their rows of sharp teeth and their rough, sandpaper-like skin, which could tear a raft.

The day came when a shark attacked. Suddenly, the raft was tossed. Callahan heard the sharp rasp of a shark rubbing against the bottom of the raft. "Keep off the bottom!" Callahan yelled, scrambling to the side as he readied his spear gun. He fired, the spear fell harmlessly into the water, and the shark swam away.

Callahan had now been on the raft for 13 days. His movements were slow, and all his thoughts focused on food. He grew weaker and weaker. Once again, Callahan aimed his speargun and shot at a fish. This time, the spear sank in. In disbelief, Callahan pulled a triggerfish aboard. His eyes filled with tears. He thought, "I weep for the fish, for me, for the state of my desperation. Then I feed on its bitter meat."

A Tiny Boat on a Large Ocean

On the 14th day, Callahan saw a ship. He launched his flares, sure the ship would see him. The ship passed Callahan and his tiny raft, and he felt a combination of despair and hope. There would be no rescue today, but if there was one ship, perhaps there would be another.

After a few days, another ship sailed past. A few days later, Callahan saw another. Each sailed by, completely unaware of the feeble flares and the desperate man waving frantically, hoping to escape his tiny raft on the huge ocean.

"My mood follows the sun," Callahan wrote. "The light of each day makes me **optimistic** that I might last another 40, but the darkness of each night makes me realize that, if any one thing goes wrong, I will not survive."

Life became routine, but it was anything but dull. Callahan tended the solar still, inspected the raft for holes, and stayed alert for fish to spear. However, his only companions were exhaustion, discomfort, and boredom. Callahan's muscles shrank because he could not exercise them. His knees looked like knots on his limp legs. The sun scorched him during the day, and at night he dreamed of food.

Vocabulary Tip
You can figure out the meaning of *optimistic* by comparing the two parts of the sentence. In the day, Callahan feels *optimistic*. However, at night he fears he may not survive. What does *optimistic* mean?

Steven Callahan after his rescue

Disaster Strikes

On the 43rd day, another disaster struck. Callahan speared a dorado. Squirming to get away, the fish ripped a hole in the bottom of the raft causing a 4-inch-long gash. Quickly, Callahan gathered his tools and tried to repair the raft. Nothing worked. Callahan ran through possible solutions in his mind. He finally decided to put a tourniquet on the area to keep it watertight, but he still had to pump up the boat.

Soon after that emergency, the dorado that Callahan hit with his spear escaped—with the spear. Callahan rooted around in his pack and found an old set of Boy Scout utensils. Perhaps he could use the knife to make a new spear. When he tried to use it, the knife blade bent. Callahan tried another knife blade. That one worked.

As the days passed, Callahan became thinner and thinner, and staying alive became more and more difficult. He couldn't think. The

Vocabulary Tip

You can figure out what *dwindled* means by thinking about the most likely thing to happen to Callahan's water supply after many days at sea.

rubber raft sprang more leaks. His water supply **dwindled**. Somehow, he forced himself to go on. His biggest battle was simply to stay awake because he was tempted to sleep until death came.

Land

On the 61st day, Callahan hit a patch of ocean pollution—clumps of oil, old bottles, fishnets—all stuck in a web of seaweed. Also stuck in the mess were tiny shrimp and crabs, which Callahan stuffed in his mouth. For the first time, the water was a lighter blue. Callahan's spirits rose. Land might be near.

More ships passed. Callahan found his mind wandering.

On the 75th night, Callahan spotted a gentle glow, which he soon realized was light from land. Excited, Callahan drank two pints of water and then told himself to calm down. He wasn't on land yet.

At dawn the next morning, Callahan's eyes filled with the sight of green plants. Callahan heard a motor and saw a boat approach with three astonished men aboard. "What islands?" Callahan motioned.

"Guadeloupe," they said. "Do you want to go to the island now?"

"No, I'm OK. I have plenty of water. I can wait. You fish. Fish!" Callahan gulped down his last five pints of water while they fished. Then the fishermen gave Callahan a piece of coconut candy. The sun set, the fishermen helped Callahan into their boat, and they towed his boat to shore. The journey was over. Callahan had survived.

After you finish reading, create your Cornell chart. Then check that you included all the major events and the important details. Add to your notes if you need to. Use your notes to write a summary of what you read.

Apply It............. To check your understanding of the story, circle the best answer to each question below.

1. The main idea of this article is that
   a. Callahan was unprepared for his trip.
   b. Callahan found ways to survive a very difficult situation.
   c. humans do not belong on the seas.
   d. Callahan was a hero.

2. Which of these did Steven Callahan *not* face during his 76-day ordeal?
   a. thirst
   b. shark attacks
   c. hunger
   d. a hurricane

3. "Soon after that emergency, the dorado that Callahan hit with his spear escaped—with the spear." In this passage, a *dorado* is:
   a. a fish.
   b. a spear.
   c. a boat.
   d. ocean pollution.

4. You can infer from this article that Steven Callahan
   a. is good at finding solutions to problems.
   b. would rather be alone than with people.
   c. does not respect the sea.
   d. often goes into situations without being well-prepared.

Test Tip

The word *best* in question 5 tells you that other words might apply. You should choose the one that best represents the way Callahan behaved in this situation.

5. When the dorado ripped a gash in the bottom of the raft, Callahan might best be described as
   a. angry.
   b. despairing.
   c. businesslike.
   d. relaxed.

Use the lines below to write your answers for numbers 6 and 7. Use your Cornell notes to help you.

6. How would you describe Steven Callahan? Use details from the story to support your writing.

_____

_____

_____

_____

_____

7. Describe Steven Callahan's most dangerous experience. Explain your choice.

_____

_____

_____

_____

_____

Lesson 2

Biography:
The Untold Stories of Louis L'Amour

Understand It......

Hint
You can review the PLAN strategy on page 12.

Louis L'Amour sold more Western stories about cowboys than anyone else in the world. It is through his life experiences that he wrote the books that entertained millions of readers. Try using the PLAN strategy to understand his biography.

Try It..............

As you preview the reading, look at the photograph, subheadings, and topic sentences. What do they tell you about the way the biography is organized? Use this information to choose a PLAN graphic. Next, begin your word map. Place check marks next to ideas or people you know something about. Put question marks next to ideas you have not heard of.

When you have finished reading, add notes to your word map about each main point. You can also add new main points that you did not predict.

Strategy Tip
You don't have to stay with your first idea for a word map. If you start drawing one and it doesn't work, try another type.

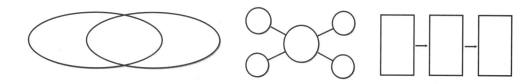

The Untold Stories of Louis L'Amour

"I had some rough times," best-selling author Louis L'Amour admitted. "I said once that *adventure* is just a romantic name for trouble. Anybody who goes looking for adventure is crazy. All of it is a lot of grief and trouble."

Those words might seem strange coming from a man who became a worldwide sensation by writing books that focus on adventure. However, Louis L'Amour was an unusual man. He left home at 15. His teenage years were difficult, L'Amour admits. "I walked by bakeries where the smell almost made me faint," he said. "A hungry man loses part of his courage. You feel like an outsider."

Strategy Tip
The topic sentences of the paragraphs on this page give you a hint that the biography is mostly written in time order. If it is, a seqence chart would work well.

The jobs L'Amour took were rough. A man in an old Ford approached him and said he needed "a tough man who can sleep on the ground and eat my cooking, and if he decides to quit it's going to be 70 miles from here and he can walk back," L'Amour remembered. The job was skinning the hides from dead cows. L'Amour took the job. It paid $3 a day. Many years later, after his "yondering years," L'Amour turned that experience into a short story. It later became his first Western novel, *Hondo*.

The "Yondering Years"
The years between skinning cows and the publication of *Hondo* were filled with experiences that shaped the stories L'Amour would later

Biography:
The Untold Stories of Louis L'Amour

write. He went to New Mexico to bale hay, wandered the West picking fruit, and worked in mines and as a lumberjack. He did whatever work he could find. This wasn't adventure, L'Amour insisted. This was survival. "I never had to steal," he said. "I've told lies, but I won't anymore. I had something else going for me during those bad years—I had the dream very young that some day I was going to make it as a writer. And I held to it." He stored away every experience and every memory to use later.

Vocabulary Tip

Sometimes you can understand a word you don't know by thinking about related words you do know. You know the word *freight* means "a load of something," so a *freighter* carries freight.

In the late 1920s, L'Amour got the urge to wander farther from home and took a **freighter** to Japan. He boxed with judo stars in Japan and then went to Shanghai, in China, to see if he could catch another ship.

In Shanghai in the 1920s, "there were 13 flags flying then, all languages were spoken," L'Amour said. There were seven or eight major warlords. Each had his own army, and each warlord was looking for soldiers. L'Amour signed up. The trail of his Asian adventures wound through Tibet, back to China, to India, and finally to Bangkok, Thailand. He returned to the United States, eager to write about where he'd been and what he'd seen, done, and learned.

Louis L' Amour

Turning Life into Stories

L'Amour wrote mystery stories, crime stories, tales about Asia, jokes, and captions—whatever would pay. However, when his book on the West, *Hondo*, became successful, he had some serious thinking to do. "Suddenly, I was a Western writer, and people wanted more Westerns," he said. L'Amour knew that many people looked at Westerns as novels about the old West when cowboys roamed the range. "If you write a story about a bygone period that takes place east of the Mississippi River, it's a historical novel. If it's west of the Mississippi, it's a Western, a different category. There's no sense to it," he said.

Vocabulary Tip

Hack means a writer who is second-best. By using the word *hack*, L'Amour says that he was not taken seriously as a writer.

"Automatically in this country, Western writing is considered low-grade writing. I had to face being considered a **hack**, and I said I'm going to go ahead and win this battle on my own terms." L'Amour won the battle. Two hundred million copies of his books are in print. They also have been translated into several languages. Thirty-one of his books have been made into movies. He became the only novelist in the United States to receive both the Congressional Gold Medal and the Presidential Medal of Freedom.

A Life without Regret

Despite the lack of respect for Westerns, L'Amour never regretted writing them or being known as a writer of Westerns. "One of the reasons I have found the West so fascinating is the kind of people who came West. The country had a way of separating men, the strong from the weak, the cowards from the brave, and this goes for the women, too. They were just as strong."

When he was in his 70s, L'Amour went back to his experiences in Asia and wrote books about those exciting days. He kept writing until the end of his life in 1988, and he produced three books every year. Despite his success, L'Amour never forgot what it was like to be lonely, hungry, and cold.

"When you sit here fat and healthy and comfortable, well, right outside your door waits cold and rain. In this world you're never safe from that, never secure. When I was broke and drifting, I would think nothing of going into a dark, empty house to find a place to sleep. Now, I'd think I was crazy to do that. I was part of that empty house then—I belonged there. I don't anymore."

After you finish reading, note what you learned by reviewing it. Write a summary, or rewrite your word map. Keep your PLAN notes and your review. They will help you remember what you have learned.

Apply It. . . . . To check your understanding of the biography, circle the best answer to each question below.

Test Tip

In question 1, all three of the adjectives must fit to make the answer correct.

1. Which series of words best describes L'Amour when he was a teenager and a young adult?
   a. angry, lonely, poor
   b. wandering, poor, dreaming
   c. angry, well-off, curious
   d. poor, unhappy, uncaring

2. L'Amour was proud of writing
   a. stories that showed the West as it really was.
   b. stories that had no good guys and bad guys.
   c. stories that showed how the West had changed.
   d. both a and b

Lesson 2 **29**

3. "He stored away every experience and every memory to use later." In that passage, the word *stored* means
   a. created.
   b. forgot.
   c. saved.
   d. threw away.

4. When L'Amour said that Western writing is considered low-grade writing, he meant that
   a. Western writing is considered just as valuable as other writing.
   b. Western writing is considered less valuable than other writing.
   c. Western writing is considered more valuable than other writing.
   d. Western writing is not for adults.

5. Throughout his life, L'Amour never forgot
   a. the people who had helped him.
   b. what being without food and a job was like.
   c. that publishers had not wanted to publish his work.
   d. that a person must depend on others.

Use the lines below to write your answers for numbers 6 and 7. Use your word map and your review to help you.

6. Write a description of Louis L'Amour based on what you learned about him in this biography.

   _____

   _____

   _____

   _____

   _____

7. Why do you think L'Amour decided to write Westerns? Use details from the biography to explain your answer.

   _____

   _____

   _____

   _____

   _____

Lesson 3

Magazine Article: Getting Lost and Loving It

Understand It......

You might not be able to tell much about this article from the title. However, by looking at the photo and previewing the article, you will see that the subject is mazes. Because you have probably solved a maze with paper and pencil, try the DRTA strategy. This strategy relies on your being able to make some predictions about what you will read.

Try It..............

First, preview the reading. Look at the title, subheadings, illustration, and topic sentences. Read the first and last paragraphs. Then make some predictions about what you will read. Next, copy the drawing of the DRTA chart below onto another sheet of paper. Write your predictions in the Preview box.

After reading, write notes about what you've read in the Take Notes box. Your notes should include supporting information for the predictions you made. If your predictions are wrong, cross them out. The Take Notes box should contain all the important points in the writing, along with the evidence or details to back up those points. When you have finished reading, write what you have learned in the Review box.

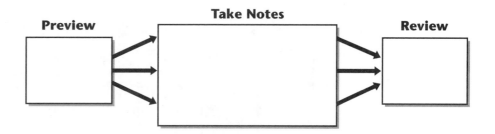

Preview → **Take Notes** → **Review**

Getting Lost and Loving It

OK, I give up. Somebody get me out of here. That is what one part of my brain tells me. The other part tells me to stand up straight and keep marching. Am I going to let a few cornstalks beat me?

I am lost in a Pennsylvania cornfield, investigating a maze so complicated that finding your way out can take more than three hours and way too much patience.

Mazes in Human History

Mazes have a long and interesting history. King Amenemhat III of Egypt created the earliest known maze about 4,000 years ago. Built in a funeral temple, the maze had nearly 3,000 rooms, some below ground and some above.

According to an ancient story, King Minos's maze, built on the Greek Island of Crete, was impossible to solve. The legend says that at the

Magazine Article:
Getting Lost and Loving It

Vocabulary Tip

In this sentence, the word *devoured* means "to eat in a greedy way."

center of the maze lived the Minotaur, a monster who **devoured** young men and young women. A young hero named Theseus made his way to the center, killed the Minotaur, and followed a golden thread back to freedom. The story may not be entirely myth. In 1900, a scientist uncovered a ruined palace on Crete that seemed to have maze-like corridors, twisting to dead ends or other rooms.

Mazes were popular throughout the Middle Ages. In 1690, one of the most famous mazes still existing was created for King William III of England. The Hampton Court maze is one-half mile of hedges too thick to see through. Many people find their way out in 15 minutes. Others become so confused that someone has to climb the ladder on the outside of the maze and provide directions.

The Hampton Court maze was the model for many others. In Victorian England, before the turn of the 20th century, about 100 mazes were planted in England. Many were destroyed, but Hampton Court still calls to puzzle-lovers. A summer visitor is likely to share the paths with another 500 mazers.

Can you solve this cornfield maze?

Mazes in American Cornfields

The idea seems to go back to 1991, when Donald Frantz saw a movie called *Field of Dreams*. In that movie, a farmer in Iowa builds a major-league baseball park in the middle of his cornfield, and people come from all over to relive their childhood baseball dreams.

The idea that cornfields could be entertaining interested Frantz. He had also recently visited some of the hedge mazes in Europe. He put the two ideas together and decided to cut a maze in a cornfield.

In 1993, Frantz cut a maze shaped like a dinosaur. Quickly, Frantz understood he had hit on a winner. In only three days, 11,000 people tried the maze. The money they paid went to help Pennsylvania flood victims.

Frantz put together the American Maze Company and began carving cornfields. In 1998, the company had seven mazes in cornfields from North Carolina to New Jersey. After years of building them, Frantz's mazes have become more and more **sophisticated**. For example, experienced maze walkers know a trick. If you keep your right hand on the wall and never lose contact with the wall, you'll quickly find the exit of some mazes. That's not true for the mazes the Maze Company builds.

So now here I am in the corn. I'm not panicked, yet. Everywhere I turn, rustling cornstalks wave gently, providing not one bit of help. To me, every cornstalk looks the same. After going through the same place for the fifth time, I give up and wave the flag on a long pole that signals the maze master, who is perched on a ladder. He uses a megaphone to offer a suggestion that seems to mock me more than it helps me. I guess I'll have to find the way out myself.

Finally, after three hours in the maze, I stumble out. It's been an entertaining afternoon in the corn, a chance to get lost and then found, but I'm ready to rest my feet and contemplate my fellow humans, many of whom find this sort of thing fun.

Vocabulary Tip

Look for clues to the meaning of *sophisticated*. Frantz's mazes don't allow people to use an easy way to find their way out. So *sophisticated* means "not simple" or "complicated."

Once you've read the article and made notes, you need to review what you've learned. Write a summary of the main points and supporting evidence in the Review box of your DRTA chart.

Apply It. . . . . To check your understanding of this article, circle the best answer to each question below.

1. The tone of this article is
   a. fun.
   b. serious.
   c. calm.
   d. angry.

2. What is the major difference between the Egyptian maze of King Amenemhat III and the Hampton Court maze?
   a. The Egyptian maze is religious, and the Hampton Court maze is not.
   b. The Egyptian maze is made of rooms in a temple, and the Hampton Court maze is made from hedges.
   c. No one was ever supposed to find the way out of the Egyptian maze.
   d. The Egyptian maze was intended only for the king, and the Hampton Court maze makes money.

3. "It's been an entertaining afternoon in the corn, a chance to get lost and then found, but I'm ready to rest my feet and contemplate my fellow humans, many of whom find this sort of thing fun." In this passage, the word *contemplate* means
   a. wander with.
   b. talk with.
   c. dismiss.
   d. think about.

4. The writer included the information about ancient mazes to
   a. show that mazes have always fascinated people.
   b. show where the cornfield maze builders got their ideas.
   c. show how boring mazes can be.
   d. both a and b

5. Donald Frantz began carving cornfields into mazes because
   a. he found the idea interesting.
   b. he liked the hedge mazes he saw in Europe.
   c. he knew people wouldn't find them entertaining.
   d. he liked the mazes he saw in Egyptian temples.

Use the lines below to write your answers for numbers 6 and 7. Use your DRTA notes to help you.

Test Tip

When a test question asks you to summarize, be sure to explain the main points and add only the most important details that explain these points.

6. Select one paragraph and summarize what it is saying.

_____

_____

_____

_____

7. Why do you think mazes fascinate people?

_____

_____

_____

_____

Arts Review:
Lesson 4 — Surprises on the Street

LANGUAGE ARTS

Understand It......

Hint
You can review the KWL Plus strategy on page 4.

This is a review of a festival of street performers called a buskerfest. Even if you have never seen a festival of buskers, or street performers, you might have seen a street musician or a mime who works for tips on the street. Because you probably know something about the subject, the KWL Plus strategy will work well for this review.

Try It...............

On another sheet of paper, draw a KWL chart like the one shown below. Think about what you know about street performers, and think about the ones you might have seen.

Write what you know in the K column. Then preview the article. Previewing may help you think about other things you know about buskers. Write those things in the K column as well.

Your next step is to write the questions you have about buskers, and about this article, in the W column. After you read, record the important information you learn and the information that answers your questions in the L column. Then write a summary of the article to help you remember what you've read. This is the "Plus" part of the strategy.

Strategy Tip

Previewing can help you write your W questions by giving you hints about what you think you are likely to learn.

K (What I know)	W (What I want to know)	L (What I've learned)

Vocabulary Tip

Troubadours might seem like a difficult word. After looking at the words and sentences around it, you might figure out that *troubadours* are poets who write songs.

Surprises on the Street

Buskers, or street performers, are similar to the **troubadours** of the Middle Ages, who told clever stories accompanied by a lute, which is a kind of guitar. The tradition of the troubadour began in France in the 11th century. At that time, troubadours were nobles and kings who wrote poems set to music. At first, they did their own singing, but in the 13th century, they hired traveling performers to do their performing for them. Through these singers, the French people heard stories of war, love, and politics.

Pantomimes who practice their art on the street today are the descendants of comic artists. Mime, or telling a story through expressions rather than words, goes back to the ancient theaters of Rome and Greece. Because there was no sound system, pantomimes had to use movements to help the audience follow the story because people could not hear any words.

Arts Review:
Surprises on the Street

The performers at the Buskerfest are modern additions to these ancient traditions. They come from all over the United States and, indeed, all over the world. They are not beggars in disguise. Most would be welcome in theaters.

Why, then, are they on the street performing in rain and wind and enduring the sneers of passers-by? According to some of the buskers, they do it because they love the freedom. Others believe there is no other place they could work.

One part of the job sets buskers aside from other performers. If a busker doesn't entertain the audience, there is no payday. That tends to create a higher level of performer. If you don't please the audience, you don't eat.

The Buskerfest is well planned, complete with a schedule so you can catch your favorite acts. Remember to bring plenty of quarters to throw into the hats of performers. Some of the buskers can become bothersome with their **pleas** for tips. Others make the plea part of their act. Although being asked for money is always annoying, somehow these buskers manage to do it and make you laugh.

There are certainly ordinary performers, like those who juggle balls and wear funny hats, but they are in the minority. Some of the performers in this Buskerfest serve up acts you shouldn't miss. Each is different and compelling. Here are some of the crowd favorites.

Zip Code Man

This performer has a most unusual act. He knows the characteristics of *every single zip code* in the United States. His act works best when audience members are from out of town. Tell him your zip code, and he'll ask if you go to a particular restaurant in that zip code. It's odd and fascinating to see how you feel when someone literally has your number. He often knows the architecture in an area and statistics about the people who live there. People who become part of his act often seem surprised, as if they've been spied on.

Molly and Ivy

These two women provide an old-fashioned juggling show complete with unicycles and flaming pins. Those of us who have watched too many boring jugglers cringe at the thought of yet another juggling act. When the juggling is well-done, though, it is a fine art. That is clear at the end of the show, when the women challenge their audience to throw them anything that will then become part of the routine. The invitation has led to their juggling skateboards, hairpins, grocery bags, and other items it wouldn't seem anyone could juggle. Somehow, Molly and Ivy do.

Vocabulary Tip

At first glance, *pleas* looks as if the word *please* was spelled wrong. However, *pleas* is a word of its own. A *plea* is a request.

Strategy Tip

You might like to ask a *how* question for your KWL chart for each of the acts described.

The Bronx Boys

These young men are remarkable to look at and remarkable to watch. They are talented gymnasts who use asphalt streets and concrete sidewalks as playgrounds for elaborate gymnastics routines. The Bronx Boys bounce off walls and one another like human rubber balls. They form towers, break them up into twists and leaps and somersaults, and then seem to fly into the next shape. They're better than most circus acts that try the same stunts—and lots more fun. They also use audience members as "props." A few minutes with this group will have you crawling back to the gym.

The One-Man Band

The one-man band is a skilled performer who can play many instruments at one time. Between the accordion on his chest, his xylophone and drums, and the dozen or so horns he has around him, this talented musician plays all of his instruments in **harmony**. The battery-operated animals seem to come alive like members of the band as they help him along with their own cymbals and drums. Sing along or suggest a tune, and the one-man band will keep playing.

How many instruments does this one-man band have?

Janice

This performer is an urban comic. She seems to love her work with the public so much that it makes sense she's on the street rather than inside a comedy club. Janice's street-based routine allows her to make the most of her wit and to comment on the passing scene as she performs her routine. Unlike some comics who make fun of people's appearance or actions, Janice never gets nasty or sets out to embarrass anyone. She'll only get into a duel of words with someone who wants to throw her off.

Man in a Box

This performer has to be seen to be believed. He looks like an ordinary guy until he begins **contorting** himself to fit into a small plastic box that wouldn't hold some people's head and shoulders. You almost

Vocabulary Tip

To figure out what *harmony* means, you can look at the words around it. Here *harmony* means "notes or instruments that sound pleasing when they are played together."

Vocabulary Tip

The word *contorting* is defined in this section. What clues can you find to its meaning?

can't believe it! He twists himself and seems to unhinge parts of his body until he packs himself inside that cube. When he's done, he looks like a pressed square of a man.

Chely, the Song Maker

Armed only with her guitar and a *very* quick wit, Chely makes up songs on the spot. To create these songs, she relies on people in the audience, who call out ideas. The lyrics weave details supplied by the audience members to create stories in which audience members star. The trick is to use the names and stories with wit to earn applause. Chely has a true gift. Some of the people who stopped to listen to her wouldn't leave to watch anyone else. Others ran to find friends to make sure they saw this wonder perform.

There are few ordinary acts at the Buskerfest. Even if you don't like mimes, give the festival a try. It's inexpensive and, if one act doesn't appeal to you, you simply move on to one that will. In this festival crowded with talent, it's a good bet that you'll be amazed by someone.

When you finish the article, complete the L column of your KWL chart. Now look back at your W questions. Were they answered? If not, answer them now. Then use your chart to write a summary of the arts review.

Apply It........... To check your understanding of the arts review, circle the best answer to each question below.

1. The main point of this article is that
   a. buskers have a hard time making a living.
   b. the Buskerfest is worth seeing.
   c. buskers are performers who are not good enough to find jobs in real shows.
   d. the buskers in the festival are like troubadours of the Middle Ages.

Test Tip

When you see the word *compare* in a question, you know you are thinking about how two things are the same.

2. Why does the author compare buskers to the troubadours of the Middle Ages?
   a. Both groups are excellent entertainers.
   b. Both groups earn their money through donations.
   c. Both groups are highly trained musicians.
   d. Both groups are sponsored by someone.

3. The sentence "If you don't please the audience, you don't eat," means
   a. if buskers don't do well, the festival won't pay them.
   b. buskers have to be friendly to be paid.
   c. people give money only to buskers who entertain them.
   d. the life of a busker is very hard.

4. "He looks like an ordinary guy, until he begins contorting himself to fit into a small plastic box that wouldn't hold some people's head and shoulders." In that sentence, the best synonym for *contorting* is
   a. damaging.
   b. sliding.
   c. bending.
   d. greasing.

5. According to this review, successful buskers
   a. are almost as good as performers in theaters.
   b. don't make any money.
   c. should avoid common themes, such as juggling.
   d. are as entertaining as traditional musicians and actors.

Use the lines below to write your answers for numbers 6 and 7. You can use your KWL chart to help you.

6. List three qualities needed to be a successful busker.

   _____

   _____

   _____

7. What does this reviewer think about buskers? Support your answer with examples.

   _____

   _____

   _____

   _____

Informative Writing:
Lesson 5 — Secrets to a Successful Job Interview

Understand It......

Hint
You can review the DRTA strategy on page 16.

This article is about how to make a job interview work for you. Maybe you or someone you know has interviewed for a job. Because you might know something about the subject, the DRTA strategy is a good choice. It helps you use what you know to understand new information.

Try It..............

When you use the DRTA strategy, you first preview the article, looking for clues about the topic. After reading the title, you can guess that the article is about helping people who go on job interviews. Preview the subheadings and you'll notice the reading is divided into three sections. These subheadings tell you how the article is organized.

Draw a DRTA chart like the one below on another sheet of paper. Write your predictions in the Preview box. Now read the article. After reading, write notes about the main points of the article in the Take Notes box. Note the evidence that supports your predictions. If your predictions are wrong, cross them off. Finally, summarize the article in the Review box.

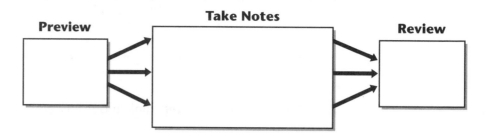

Preview → Take Notes → Review

Secrets to a Successful Job Interview

Almost everyone will interview for a job sooner or later. The experience can be frightening, but there are some techniques for successful interviewing that make your chance of success greater. A successful interviewee prepares for the interview, behaves well during the interview, and follows up after the interview.

Prepare

If you have been offered an interview, you have **jumped the first hurdle**. Before the interview itself, you need to take some steps.

Find out as much as you can about the company that is interviewing you. It may have brochures or an annual report. The company may also have a site on the World Wide Web. Try doing some research there. While a small company or a retail shop may have no printed material, you can often find out about them by talking to people who work there.

Vocabulary Tip

The phrase *jumped the first hurdle* is a figure of speech. To understand this expression, think about who usually jumps hurdles: racehorses and runners. When you *jump the first hurdle*, you successfully begin the race.

Next, review information about yourself. That may seem unnecessary since you know who you are. However, you need to think about how a prospective employer will see you. The best way to prepare is to write your answers to some often-asked questions.

Most employers will ask about your work and school history. They may want examples of how you handled yourself in difficult situations. They may ask what your career goals are and why you want the job. They may ask why they should hire you. You can guess at other questions when you think about the job for which you are applying.

After you have thought about your answers, ask a friend, teacher, parent, or another adult to interview you as practice.

Before you go to the interview, make sure you are properly groomed and dressed. Avoid clothes that would not be appropriate in the workplace. Never chew gum or carry something to drink. Take a pad of paper, a pencil, and extra copies of your résumé. Depending on the job, take along samples of your writing or artwork.

Present Yourself

Never be late to an interview. According to research, most employers make up their minds about hiring someone during the first five minutes of an interview, so the first impression is important. When you are introduced, shake hands firmly, look directly at the interviewer, and offer a warm smile.

Enthusiasm for the job and a positive attitude are real assets. If two people are equally qualified, the one who really seems to want the job will get it. Employers want to hire people who make their job easier. They want people who can see what needs to be done and do it. When you respond to questions, answer in complete sentences. "Yes" and "no" do not give an employer an idea of who you are and what you can do. On the other hand, if you know that you talk too much when you're nervous, practice answering questions fully and completely and then being quiet.

One trick that may help you on an interview is to keep in mind three or four qualities about yourself that you feel make you an excellent person for the job. Be specific. Instead of saying you are a **self-starter**, for example, explain how you saw something specific that needed to be done and how you did it. That kind of detail will impress an employer. Interviewers commonly end interviews by asking if you have questions. Use this chance to bring up important points about yourself that were not already discussed. You might say, "I do have a question. But before I ask it, may I mention a couple of things?"

Avoid asking about benefits and salary. If you are offered the job, you will find out that information then. Instead, ask questions that show

Informative Writing:
Secrets to a Successful Job Interview

that you understand the company and the job. You might ask about chances for promotion or how the responsibilities of the job might change as you work there.

End the interview with a firm handshake and another smile. If no one has said anything about contacting you, ask what the next steps are and tell the interviewer again how much you would like the job. You can also say, "May I contact you about this job in a week?"

Follow Up

The first thing you should do after you leave is take notes, especially if you are interviewing for more than one job. You don't want to become confused about which employer said what. Write what you learned about the job, how you liked the people, what they told you about the workplace, and when you can expect to hear from them.

The next thing to do is write a thank-you letter. It should be no longer than a page. Discuss how much you would like the job and how much you enjoyed the interview and the chance to find out more about the company. Restate what you could offer the company as an employee and how your skills and abilities suit you for the job. If you are not sure how to spell any of the names, call and find out. The employer will think you pay attention to details.

If you said you would call on a certain day, call. If you have done everything right, chances are you will get the job.

Strategy Tip

Before you take notes, look over what you have read. The subheadings can remind you of important information.

When you finish reading and taking notes, look over your DRTA chart to make sure you understand what you've written. Then write a summary of the selection in the Review box.

Apply It............ To check your understanding of the article, circle the best answer to each question below.

Test Tip

Although several of the answers in question 1 might be points made in the article, only one is the *main* idea.

1. The main idea of this article is that
    a. you can get a job if you know how to present yourself during an interview.
    b. if you prepare for an interview, know how to handle yourself, and follow up afterward, your chances of getting a job are better.
    c. enthusiasm is the most important part of interviewing because if two candidates are equal, the employer will hire the enthusiastic one.
    d. the first impression you make when you are being interviewed will often determine whether you get the job.

2. When you prepare for an interview, you should
   a. research how much money people who are in similar jobs make.
   b. find out as much about the company as you can.
   c. both a and b
   d. neither a nor b

3. "You need to think about how a prospective employer will see you, though." In this sentence, the word *prospective* means
   a. possible.
   b. considered.
   c. informed.
   d. considerate.

4. According to this article, someone who wants a job should *not*
   a. show up in a suit.
   b. show how much he or she wants the job.
   c. ask about salary or benefits.
   d. bring samples of his or her work.

5. You can infer that one reason to write a thank-you letter is to
   a. take another opportunity to talk about your strong points.
   b. prove that you are polite.
   c. show that other employers want you, too.
   d. prove that you can write a letter.

Use the lines below to write your answers for numbers 6 and 7. Use your DRTA notes to help you.

6. Make a list of four important things to do as you prepare for a successful job interview.

_____

_____

_____

_____

7. Think of a job that sounds interesting to you. Describe the job. Then write three things about yourself that could convince someone to hire you for that job.

_____

_____

_____

_____

Unit 2 Review
Reading in Language Arts

In this unit, you have practiced using the KWL Plus, Cornell Note-taking, PLAN, and DRTA strategies. Choose one strategy and use it when you read the selection below. Use a separate sheet of paper to draw charts, take notes, and summarize what you learn.

Hint *Remember that all reading strategies have activities for before, during, and after reading. To review these steps, look back at Unit 1 or at the last page of this book.*

Gawky Girl Makes Good

"Every time someone asks me to sign a book, I feel like laughing," says Sandra Cisneros. "It's so wacky. I was the girl with the Cs and Ds. I was the girl in the corner with the goofy glasses from Sears. I was the ugly kid in the class with the bad haircut, the one nobody would talk to. I was the one that never got picked to be in the play."

It was difficult going from a shy, poor, uncertain child to a nationally celebrated author. Cisneros kept her writing secret when she was a child in Chicago in the 1960s. "If you came from the neighborhood I came from, you had to hide everything that mattered to you," she says.

Her family had emigrated from Mexico and traveled back and forth from Mexico to the United States during her childhood. The constant movement was upsetting to Cisneros, who escaped to the library.

With the support of her parents, Cisneros went to college and graduated. From there, she went to the celebrated Iowa Writers'

Workshop, which has hosted some of the nation's best writers.

She was not like the others there. Many were from well-off families. "They had been bred as hothouse flowers," Cisneros says. "I was a yellow weed among the city's cracks." That difference, she decided, was not a problem. Instead, it defined who she was. "That's when I decided I would write about something my classmates couldn't write about," she says.

The result was her first book, *The House on Mango Street*, a rich poetic look at Cisneros's youth through the eyes of another shy, uncertain girl. The book was a hit, and Cisneros was hailed as a brilliant new writer.

Even as the book gained her admirers, Cisneros was struggling. The year her first book of poetry was published, she couldn't find work. She believed she was a failure.

Finally, a literary agent sold a book of Cisneros's short stories to a major publisher. Most of the book had yet to be written, though. "There's nothing like a deadline to teach you discipline," Cisneros says.

The book, *Woman Hollering Creek*, was published to rave reviews. Cisneros found herself becoming a celebrity. She could finally afford to write full-time.

Despite her success, Cisneros is passionate about remembering

where she came from. "I think about who I was, a quiet person who was never asked to speak in class and never picked for anything, and how I am finding that with words I have the power to make people listen, to make them think in a new way, to make them cry, to make them laugh. It's a powerful thing to make people listen to you."

Use your notes and chart to help you answer the questions below.

1. Cisneros kept her writing secret when she was a child because
   a. her parents did not believe that was a way for a girl to spend her time.
   b. she came from a neighborhood that would not have appreciated her writing.
   c. her friends had told her not to bother with her writing.
   d. she wrote in Spanish.

2. Cisneros called her fellow writers at the Iowa Writers' Workshop "hothouse flowers" because
   a. they felt superior to her, with her poor background.
   b. they didn't care about the world of the poor.
   c. they were college-educated, and she was not.
   d. they were from well-off backgrounds, unlike her.

3. You can conclude that Cisneros has become a successful writer because
   a. she makes her stories real and interesting to readers.
   b. most readers had the same upbringing she did.
   c. students are required to read her work.
   d. she has always had the support of the literary world.

4. Explain why Cisneros is surprised by the praise she has received.

_____

_____

5. Describe Cisneros's feelings about her writing.

_____

_____

Unit 3
Reading in Social Studies

Most of the reading you do is probably connected with social studies. At school, you read about history, geography, and government. You also may read about sociology and economics. At home, you read newspapers and magazines about what is happening in the world. This is social studies reading, too. You even do social studies reading when you read about a trip you will be taking. That is how you learn what to pack and what to expect when you reach your destination. Reading in social studies is a skill you will use often.

How Social Studies Reading Is Organized

Although social studies subjects differ greatly, there are some patterns you can learn to identify. Recognizing these patterns will help you understand what you read. You will be better prepared to fit together what you already know with what you will be learning. Here are some common ways social studies text is organized. You may see a combination of these patterns in one selection.

Main Idea and Details. This pattern is probably the most common in social studies. Within the reading, the topic will have several main ideas. Each of these main ideas will have details that explain and support it. Below is an example of how this might look as a picture:

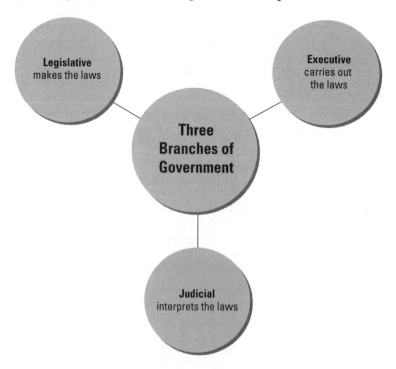

Cause and Effect. Major events in history may cause many later events. Sometimes social studies texts present history as a series of causes and effects. Creating boxes that show causes and effects can help you organize your information. Here is an example of the way this pattern might look:

Irish Immigration to the United States

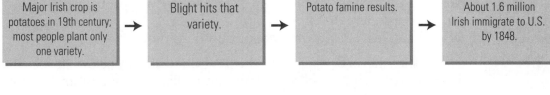

Cause
Major Irish crop is potatoes in 19th century; most people plant only one variety. →

Effect (New Cause)
Blight hits that variety. →

Effect (New Cause)
Potato famine results. →

Effect (New Cause)
About 1.6 million Irish immigrate to U.S. by 1848.

Sequence of Events. Some social studies texts are written in chronological, or time, order. Others describe a series of steps. You may notice this pattern when you see dates as you preview. Timelines or a series of boxes can help you understand this pattern. Sometimes the series of events is a process, as in the following example:

How a Bill Becomes Law

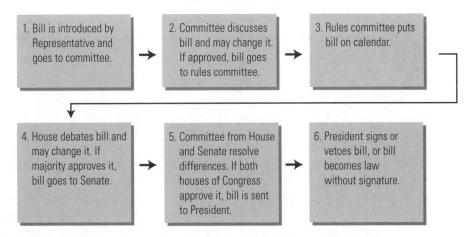

1. Bill is introduced by Representative and goes to committee. →

2. Committee discusses bill and may change it. If approved, bill goes to rules committee. →

3. Rules committee puts bill on calendar.

4. House debates bill and may change it. If majority approves it, bill goes to Senate. →

5. Committee from House and Senate resolve differences. If both houses of Congress approve it, bill is sent to President. →

6. President signs or vetoes bill, or bill becomes law without signature.

Getting the Most from Your Reading

If you can recognize the way a text is organized, you will be better prepared to learn new information. Making drawings like these can help you understand—and remember—what you read.

Lesson 6

Civics: Should Women Vote?

Understand It......

Hint

You can review the KWL Plus strategy on page 4.

This selection is about the debate over whether women should have the right to vote. People throughout the country argued about the issue in the late 1800s and early 1900s. In 1919, the 19th Amendment to the Constitution gave women the right to vote. You probably know something about women's struggle to vote. That makes KWL Plus a good reading strategy to use to understand the debate.

Try It..............

The speeches below were given by women around 1900. From the title, you know you will probably be reading a debate. People will present opposing opinions. You can also guess that the speeches will probably not be about the history of the issue. Each speaker will probably try to convince listeners that her opinion is correct. When you preview, try to recall what you already know about both opinions.

Strategy Tip

As you form your questions for the KWL chart, consider what you will read. In this selection, for example, questions about history may not be answered. However, questions about the arguments for and against women's suffrage probably will be answered.

On another sheet of paper, copy the KWL chart shown below. In the K column, write what you already know and what you thought of when you previewed the speeches. Write what you want to know in the W section. Then read the speeches. As you do, look for the information that answers your questions. Write the important points you learned in the L section. After you read, use your KWL chart to summarize both speakers' opinions.

K (What I know)	W (What I want to know)	L (What I've learned)

Vocabulary Tip

Suffragists are people who believe in women's *suffrage,* or women's right to vote.

Should Women Vote?

Taken from records at the New York Century Club, 1901

AGAINST: Mrs. Julia M. Shaw

Gentlemen: I stand before you today, a woman proud to be a homemaker, a wife, and a mother. I fill my days serving those I love. I think only of their welfare. I am distressed at the **suffragists** who would force upon me a radical change in the way society sees me and in the way I see the world. Allow me to explain why I firmly believe that our current system—which has served us well for hundreds of years—should stand.

Women are not meant for the affairs of the world. We are meant to deal with the affairs of the heart and of the home. That is where our interest is and where our interest should be. I have no desire to change places with my husband and wear his trousers. I wish to devote my time and energy to the affairs that matter to me. If I were to devote my time instead to the affairs of state that concern him, my attention would be diverted. That would not be good for my family or for me. On a larger scale, such a diversion of women's attention would not be good for the nation. Women have always been devoted to the home, not to the greater affairs outside the home. If we direct our attention outside the home, our families will suffer as will the entire structure of society.

What is more, I do not have the information to make the decisions voting would thrust upon me. I do not spend my days reading great tomes, nor do I spend my days in deep discussion of world affairs. How am I to know the correct vote? Far better to leave that to the husbands of the world, who are willing to **shoulder that burden** for us women. They are equipped for it. We are not.

I also would hesitate to vote knowing that I could send men to war to die but could not go myself. War is men's work. However, if women were granted the right to vote, they would be voting to direct others to go to wars on foreign ground and die for them. That right, if one wishes to call it that, is not one I would choose to exercise.

Why force the vote on a population that has no desire to have it? In Massachusetts in 1895, women were asked if they wanted the vote. Only 5 percent said yes. Women don't want change.

These suffragettes who claim to represent us do not. They are women who bully, women who are unladylike. They are bitter women who are outside the mainstream of society and who apparently want to be men.

In Kansas in 1887, women were given the right to vote on local issues. Since then, the vote for women has not been extended. Women still cannot vote in other elections. If women's suffrage works, why have these rights not been further extended? The answer is that voting by women does not work well, and women *do not want this right!*

Allow us to return to the gracious days when women were able to live the lives they were intended to live. We do not want to be men. We want to be women. Allow us that right.

FOR: Mrs. Charlotte Ramsey

Women suffragettes are no more than true daughters of the Revolution. We believe what our founders believed in and the principles for which they fought and died. We believe in equality. We believe that women, as much as men, have the right to make decisions about their government.

Why should we not have this right? We are thinking, breathing, intelligent people. What is strange about the current debate is who the anti-suffragist movement believes should vote and who should not. Our schoolteachers are mostly women. Yet such women, many of them college educated, are not considered the intellectual equals of men who

Civics:
Should Women Vote?

can neither read nor write, men who might have had no more than a year or two of school. I ask you, who is the better decision-maker likely to be?

Women demonstrate (in a march through New York City) in 1912 for the right to vote.

We women who ask for the vote are like our Revolutionary brothers in another way. We do not believe in taxation without representation. That is exactly what is happening today. Many women, both married and single, own property and pay taxes on it. Yet those women have no say in the taxes they must pay. That issue led to the Revolutionary War. We do not intend to fight, but we do intend to seek the one thing that can change this disgraceful situation. We want to vote.

Women must also obey laws they do not agree with but that govern them. Times have changed. Not all women have the protection of a man or a family. They take care of themselves. Laws designed to protect women, laws that govern the jobs they may hold, are based on the idea that every woman has the protection and economic support of a man. Women who must depend on themselves often suffer.

Some people say women are not **fit** to vote because they live in the shelter of the home and have no experience of the world. That is not true now, if it ever was. Women graduate from college, they read, and they think. Many work and earn money. They certainly have the knowledge and desire to participate in the country's life. Women are fit to be partners in the enterprise of government.

Women are more than just fit partners in government; they are essential partners. Women's point of view should be part of the discussion. Women plan for the future of children. They understand domestic issues in ways that men cannot. Women might be hesitant to send our sons to war—but is that the position of a weaker sex or the position of a sex responsible for the good health of its offspring? Perhaps if women had voted, some needless wars might have been avoided. Women offer a perspective critical to balanced public debate.

Women should have the vote. We—and the country—deserve no less!

Vocabulary Tip

You probably know a few definitions for *fit*. You know that when a shirt *fits*, it's the right size. You may also know another meaning for fit; "to be qualified for." Which meaning makes sense here?

After you have finished reading, write what you have learned in the L section of your KWL chart. Make sure you included all the important points of both speakers. Use your chart to write a summary that will help you remember what you read.

Apply It............ To check your understanding of the debate, circle the best answer to each question.

1. Which argument does Mrs. Shaw make against women's suffrage?
   a. Women are not smart enough to vote.
   b. Women are too emotional to vote.
   c. Women are not meant to deal with affairs of state.
   d. all of the above

2. When Mrs. Shaw says that she does not want to wear her husband's trousers, she means
   a. she wants to wear frilly dresses.
   b. she does not want her husband to feel less important.
   c. people will think she is a suffragist if she wears his trousers.
   d. she does not want to take on what she thinks of as a male role.

3. "I do not spend my days reading great tomes, nor do I spend my days in deep discussion of world affairs." In this sentence, the word *tomes* means
   a. remarks.
   b. ideas.
   c. books
   d. maps.

4. You can infer that Mrs. Ramsey mentioned the American Revolution because
   a. she wanted to connect the Revolution and women's suffrage.
   b. she wanted men to feel ashamed that women could not vote.
   c. she wanted her listeners to feel patriotic.
   d. she knew there would be veterans in the audience.

5. The two speakers differ on the issue of
   a. whether women are smart enough to vote.
   b. whether women should be married.
   c. whether women want to be involved in national affairs.
   d. whether women should have children.

Use the lines below to write your answers for numbers 6 and 7. Use your KWL notes to help you.

Test Tip

You should already have a good summary you can use to help you answer question 6.

6. Write a few sentences that describe this debate.

_____

_____

7. How do you think having the right to vote could change the way a person thinks about himself or herself?

_____

_____

_____

Lesson 6   **51**

Lesson 7

Geography:
Journey Down the Unknown River

Understand It......

Hint
You can review the PLAN strategy on page 12.

This article is about the exploration of the Colorado River. Because you might not know about the topic, the PLAN strategy is a good choice. When you use the PLAN method, you think about how the article is organized and then design a word map. Then you record your notes on the word map after you read.

Try It..............

Preview the article. Look at the subheadings, the first and last paragraphs, and the topic sentences. While you preview, try to get an idea of how the article is organized. Is it written in chronological, or time, order? If it is, a sequence chart might work best. Is it about one main subject? Then a wheel-and-spoke diagram might work. If the article compares two things, you might use a Venn diagram. Copy one of the graphics below onto another sheet of paper or create your own graphic.

Once you choose a graphic, predict what the article will be about. Write your predictions in the graphic. Next, locate information by looking at what you predicted. Place check marks next to ideas you know something about and question marks next to unknown ideas. After you read the article, add information to the map. Finally, summarize the article.

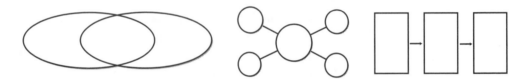

Strategy Tip
You may want to change your reading speed based on how many check marks and how many question marks you wrote. The more you need to understand, the slower you should read.

Journey Down the Unknown River

On maps, the only label was "unexplored." About 300 miles wide and 500 miles long, the entire Colorado Plateau region in Utah and Arizona was a mystery to mapmakers. The Colorado River flowed through it and no one had traveled the length of the river and survived. In 1869, John Wesley Powell set out to learn more about the mighty Colorado.

Powell, although inexperienced, had long wanted to be the first to explore the Grand Canyon by boat. In 1869, Powell talked his wartime friend, President Ulysses S. Grant, into allowing Powell and his crew to take food from government posts in the West. Armed with the presidential order for food, Powell and his crew began their journey.

Powell packed his wooden boats tightly. He thought the group might be on the river ten months. Each of the three large boats carried 2,000 pounds of supplies. A smaller fourth boat would serve as a scout boat. The nine-member crew was eager but apprehensive. No one knew whether the explorers would be able to find a way out once they were on the river in the Grand Canyon. People had told fearful tales of the Grand Canyon and the river that ran through it. They spoke of thundering waterfalls, whirlpools that plunged people to their deaths, and impossible rapids.

Strategy Tip
When you preview and look at a photograph or an illustration, make sure to read the caption, too. Captions sometimes point to important ideas in an article.

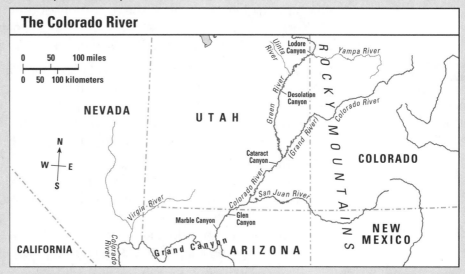

The Colorado River

Powell's crew traveled 240 miles down the Colorado River.

On the River

The expedition left on May 24, 1869, from Green River, Colorado. The swift current swept the boats downstream. For 60 miles, the boats traveled swiftly but **uneventfully**. There were no high canyons and no rapids.

At the first sight of rapids, the party stopped and spent three days measuring the height of the cliffs and taking scientific notes. Then the boats plunged into what Powell named Horseshoe Canyon. The first rapid scared them and then thrilled them as they ran it successfully.

The walls of the canyon got steeper by the minute. The river narrowed, and the rapids became more violent. Because the rapids could be frightening, the men preferred running them with a slower but safer plan. The boats were first unloaded, attached to a rope, and led gently over the falls or the rapid by the crew. Then the crew carried the tons of supplies around to meet the boat.

After going through a fierce rapid the crew named the Canyon of Lodore, the crew of one of the boats struggled to make shore. Horrified, the rest of the men watched as the boat hurtled over a steep fall and then struck a boulder. The men were flung out and swept helplessly down the river. The boat smashed on the rocks below. The men were rescued, but all the food on the boat, as well as the equipment, was lost.

The next misfortune occurred when the crew built a cooking fire too close to some willow trees, and the fire burned the crew's camping spot. After that, life was calm for a time. On June 18, the crew members floated past the spot where the Yampa River flows into the Green River,

Vocabulary Tip
The word *uneventfully* has several parts. It has a base word, *event*; a prefix, *un-*, which means "not"; and a suffix, *-fully*, which means "full of." Put the word parts together to define the word: "not full of events," or "smoothly."

Geography:
Journey Down the Unknown River

and the water is swift and smooth. They traveled through the wide, slow section of the Green where the Uinta River runs. The canyon walls became higher and higher, the rock more and more barren. At one point, rapids pitched several men out of their boat. With the help of two other men, Powell managed to save himself and the boat.

At the stretch of the river called Desolation Canyon, the crew found one rapid after another. Then came 18 miles of small rapids made up of swift, sparkling water that the men enjoyed running. At the site of what is now Green River, Utah, they passed one of the few known crossings of the river. On the afternoon of July 16, they met the Grand River.

On the Grand and the Colorado

On July 21, the group members floated into the Colorado River. Although the Colorado had gentle stretches, it also had terrifying rapids. Some were in canyons too narrow to walk the supplies around. More than once, they shot down a blind waterfall, sure they were plunging to their deaths. They named that stretch of rapids Cataract Canyon.

The next challenge was Marble Canyon, one of the most dangerous stretches of the river. The river squeezed between the flinty rocks, and the rapids pounded the boats. The walls grew higher and higher, reaching 3,000 feet up to the canyon rim. Powell demanded they spend two days repairing the boats.

Powell feared the stretch ahead. "We have an unknown distance yet to run; an unknown river yet to explore," he wrote. In reality, 217 miles lay ahead, and then calm water. Before the easy water, though, lay a terrible stretch of rapids.

On August 27, with about five days worth of food left, the party came upon what they thought of as the most dangerous rapid yet. One man called it "a hell of foam." Powell climbed the canyon walls to take a look at the rapid. He could see no way to walk around it. It was, one man wrote, "the darkest day of the trip."

After three crew members abandoned the trip, the rest of the crew got back on the river, straining to beat the furious water. They went down the falls, broke into the waves, and rowed desperately for shore. Several rapids later, the boats floated into calm water. When they reached the mouth of the Virgin River on August 30, the men saw a group of Native Americans fishing. The men had made it. They were the first to travel through the Grand Canyon by boat.

Strategy Tip
This section discusses the rapids on the Colorado. Add these facts to your word map.

Strategy Tip
This section discusses another danger the crew faced—a shortage of food. Add this information to your word map.

Strategy Tip
When you write a summary, check how well you understood what you have read.

Look at your PLAN notes. Did you include all the main points and details? Note your understanding by writing a summary or using another method to review your reading. If you'd prefer, you can write your summary in the form of a news story or a journal.

Apply It............ To check your understanding of the article, circle the best answer to each question below.

1. Which of these hardships did Powell and his crew face on their trip?
   a. angry landowners
   b. lack of food
   c. poorly built boats
   d. flash floods

2. You can infer that Powell wanted to run the river because
   a. he was adventurous.
   b. he wanted exciting objects for his museum.
   c. he wanted the government to take notice of his talents.
   d. he wanted to prove to President Grant that he could do it.

3. "The nine-member crew was eager but apprehensive. . . . People had told fearful tales of the Grand Canyon. . . ." In this passage, *apprehensive* means
   a. busy.
   b. fearful.
   c. prepared.
   d. unwilling.

4. John Wesley Powell can best be described as
   a. foolish and brave.
   b. determined and brave.
   c. cautious and scientific.
   d. independent and commanding.

Test Tip

When a test question asks you to *infer* an answer, think about what you have read. Which of these choices seems most logical?

5. You can infer that the last major rapid the men faced
   a. was more frightening because they were homesick.
   b. could have been walked around if the men had been stronger.
   c. was so dangerous because the boats were damaged.
   d. looked more dangerous because the men were exhausted and hungry.

Use the lines below to write your answers for numbers 6 and 7. Use your PLAN notes to help you.

6. Suppose that you are Powell. Explain to President Grant why he should support your trip.

_____

_____

7. What might you have found most difficult about the trip?

_____

_____

Lesson 8

Sociology: Living at the Mall

Understand It......

Hint

You can review the DRTA strategy on page 16.

This article is about the role of the modern shopping mall in U.S. society. You probably know a few things about shopping malls. Try the DRTA strategy with this reading because it works well when you are familiar with the topic. You should be able to preview the article and make predictions about the kind of information you will learn.

Try It..............

Below is a drawing of the DRTA chart. Copy it onto another sheet of paper. When you use the DRTA strategy, you first preview the reading, looking for clues about what the article will contain. You already know this reading is about shopping malls. Based on what you see when you preview, make predictions. Write your predictions in the Preview box.

Then read the article, checking to see if your predictions are correct. If they are, write the evidence that supports them in the Take Notes box. If your predictions are wrong, cross them off and write the points you did not predict. When you have finished reading, you will summarize what you have learned in the Review box.

Strategy Tip

When you preview, you add what you learn to what you already know to make predictions.

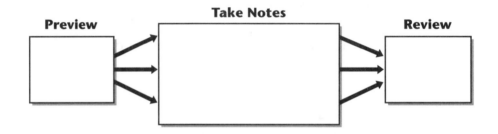

Preview   Take Notes   Review

Strategy Tip

Think about the subheadings. What do you know about these topics? Use this information to predict what you will learn. You can also use the subheadings to review.

Living at the Mall

Shopping malls are a part of almost every community. Once people spent time at the town square or on Main Street. Today, the shopping mall is the new town square.

For many decades, a town square surrounded by shops was the center of many communities. The lawns and sidewalks and parks also belonged to the community. Such spaces included not only stores but also post offices, community and government offices, libraries, and, perhaps, a town auditorium. Town squares became centers because people went there for many reasons, from mailing packages to returning library books. Along the way, they met neighbors. People stopped and discussed news, community issues, and national affairs. Town squares often served as centers for other community events, such as band concerts or holiday ceremonies.

The History of the Shopping Center

Then along came the shopping center. Since the 1920s, when the idea of a central shopping area first developed, a shopping-center design has gone through several stages. The first stage, which appeared in California in the 1920s and 1930s, was the result of a new invention: the car. Developers bought a piece of land, provided plenty of parking spaces, and grouped together several stores.

In the 1950s and 1960s, shopping malls grew with the suburbs. In most cases, suburbs had no town squares. Suburbs often had no large groups of stores. Developers created larger groups of stores. By then, however, planners had had time to do some thinking about the arrangement of stores. Developers knew that a major department store or two would attract customers. Those stores could be at either end of an area that housed many smaller stores. To get from one major store to the other, shoppers would have to walk past many smaller stores.

These malls were quite different from town squares. In towns, store owners often owned the land their stores were built on. Shopping centers changed that. A developer owned all the land and made all the rules. The developer often set hours for the stores, chose the tenants, and enforced rules about how stores could look.

Stores in the first shopping centers all had outside entrances but often faced inward as well. This inward side was a small self-contained world. Shopping center owners didn't want shoppers to think about the world outside. They wanted people to focus on shopping, and people did.

Enclosed malls **disconnected** people from the outside world even more. People inside an air-conditioned mall didn't need to think about the world outside. They only needed to concentrate on the opportunity to spend money.

In recent years, developers have followed the trend to create "shopping experiences." In Colorado, one Denver mall calls itself a "retail resort." From cozy leather chairs to wooden log walls, the design says "dude ranch." However, this dude ranch is entirely devoted to shopping, not to the great outdoors.

Should Malls Be More Than Just Stores?

As small towns saw their main streets die and as suburban residents wondered where their childhood meeting places had gone, complaints about malls grew. Malls were soulless places devoted to greed instead of to the common good. Malls told young people that the best place to be was a place where they could spend money.

Some planners and community activists say it is too late to save many downtowns. They think that the mall serves the same purpose as the town square did.

Dr. Judith Coady, a professor at the University of Connecticut, told *The New York Times* that she began to study shopping malls as community

---

Vocabulary Tip

You can understand *disconnected* by looking at the parts of the word. The prefix *dis-* means "the opposite of." The base word *connect* means "to join." The suffix *-ed* shows that something happened in the past. So *disconnected* means "not joined."

centers. She found out that she was wrong. "I expected to find the mall as some kind of new community," she said. "But I found that the mall is not a community at all. . . . The focus is on consumption, on the pleasure of just being there. The issues that are part of our everyday community are not discussed there, so it isn't a community."

Coady watched people at the mall and found that they walked differently inside than they did outside. "It's a slower walk to the rhythm of music in the mall," she said. "The eyes are unfocused. Generally speaking, there's a kind of glaze in the eyes. The mall brings it on."

Because people are with others in the mall, she said that they feel like they are part of a community. "However, as people wander in the malls," she said, "community problems get worse. While people are dallying in the malls, the problems remain hidden and out of sight." Some planners are trying to build suburbs based on a town square design, but much of America meets at malls. Can malls become more than just huge groups of stores?

The Walt Whitman Center at Rutgers University is working on a project to turn shopping malls into more active areas of communities. It is bringing new elements to malls, such as community theaters, public-health centers, day-care centers, public libraries, or playgrounds. "If malls are the only public spaces left to us in many parts of the country, they must become more like real towns," the project leaders wrote. If business is not to become the **sole** public activity we engage in, we must offer alternative activities—civic, cultural, athletic, political, and recreational—that define us as citizens as well as consumers."

Developers and mall owners who are happy with the way malls are may not want to add those elements. Some developers, though, welcome the idea. A mall in Massachusetts has a library, a church, and a home for senior citizens. In Silver Spring, Maryland, a developer is creating a mall that will serve as a town square. It will continue to bring people together in a place where they feel safe. At the same time, they can enjoy themselves and various recreational activities.

The future mall may be different from today's malls. Imagine a mall that serves as a town square, where people meet to talk, check out library books, and listen to debates and concerts. The mall we have known for decades does not have to be the mall of the future.

Vocabulary Tip

The word *sole* has several different meanings—"a fish," "the bottom of a shoe," and "only." You can figure out which one fits by looking at the rest of the sentence.

After you finish taking notes in your DRTA chart, look over what you have written. Add other important ideas or details. Then write a summary of the article. That will help you remember what you have read.

Apply It.. . . . . To check your understanding of the article, circle the best answer to each question below.

1. The main idea of this article is that
   a. shopping malls have replaced town squares.
   b. shopping malls are good places to shop.
   c. shopping malls are becoming larger and larger.
   d. both b and c

2. According to the article, developers began enclosing malls because
   a. they did not want customers to think about the outside world.
   b. they did not want customers to feel uncomfortable.
   c. the store owners demanded it.
   d. they wanted to make shopping pleasant.

3. " 'However, as these people wander in the malls,' she said, 'community problems get worse. While people are dallying in the malls, the problems remain hidden and out of sight.' " In this passage, the word *dallying* means
   a. spending time.
   b. working.
   c. hiding out.
   d. eating.

4. Judith Coady learned through her research that
   a. malls serve as community centers.
   b. people want malls to be more like community centers.
   c. developers plan to make malls more like community centers.
   d. people at malls uncorrectly feel they are part of a community.

5. Developers might not want a mall to be more like a town square because
   a. developers might not want to spend money to change the mall.
   b. people might not come to the mall.
   c. developers would not want disagreements in the mall.
   d. developers would not want to give out social services.

Use the lines below to write your answers for numbers 6 and 7. Use your DRTA notes to help you.

Test Tip

Question 6 has two parts. You must tell *both* how town squares and shopping malls are the same and how they are different.

6. How are town squares and shopping malls similar? How are they different?

_____

_____

7. What is the author's opinion of malls? Use examples from the article to support your ideas.

_____

_____

History:
Lesson 9   A Fever in the Land

Understand It......

Hint

You can review the KWL Plus strategy on page 4.

You've probably heard of the Salem witch trials. In the 17th century, young girls accused people in the Massachusetts village of Salem of being witches. KWL Plus is a good reading strategy for history because you link what you already know to what you learn when you read.

Try It...............

Draw a KWL chart like the one below on another sheet of paper. Then think about what you know about the Salem witch trials and preview the selection. Look at the first and last paragraphs, the illustration, the subheadings, and the topic sentences. In the K column, write key words and phrases that say what you know already. Then write the questions you have about the subject in the W column. After you read, fill in the L section with the information you learn. Your last step will be to write a summary of what you have learned.

Strategy Tip

If you find that what you have written in the K column is not correct, revise it. That way, you won't become confused later.

K (What I know)	W (What I want to know)	L (What I've learned)

A Fever in the Land

It started innocently enough in 1692, with a game of fortunetelling. By the end of this terrible time in U.S. history, 20 people had been killed. After an eight-month ordeal, the terror ended.

The Sin of Telling Fortunes

In 1692, children had little to do in Salem Village, Massachusetts. The society was strictly Puritan. Girls stayed inside during the winter, doing chores and reading the Bible. During that winter, the minister's daughter, Betty Parris, age 9, and her cousin Abigail Williams, age 11, amused themselves by listening to the stories of Tituba, an enslaved woman from the West Indies.

Tituba told the folktales of her native land to the girls and several of their friends. She also taught them fortune-telling games, such as dropping an egg white into a glass of water to foretell the job that a future husband would have.

While playing that game, Betty felt guilty because her strict society did not permit such games. As a result of her guilt, Betty believed that she saw a coffin in the water. She began moaning and writhing on the floor like a snake. Soon, Abigail joined her. Alarmed, their friends called the village doctor, William Griggs. He looked at the girls and offered his diagnosis: witchcraft.

Soon other girls began behaving strangely. They screamed and shouted and refused to say their prayers. Witches had caused this, people thought, and the girls had a duty to name them.

Finally, the girls gave the names of people who fit the Puritans' idea of witches. They named as witches three women who were generally disliked. The women did not belong to well-known families, and they had little money or influence. One was Tituba, the enslaved woman. Another was Sarah Goode, a homeless beggar. The third was Sarah Osborne, who had been accused of witchcraft several years earlier.

The Trials Begin

The women were arrested and questioned by the town judges. The girls who had accused them were also in the room. As the women began to answer the judges' questions, the girls again began writhing on the floor.

After her owner, the Reverend Samuel Parris, beat her, Tituba confessed. She described how she rode through the air on a stick to attend meetings of the witches.

The girls named other witches, accusing even well-respected people in the village. At this time, opinions about Reverend Parris's leadership of the church divided the community. Several people had refused to pay their share of his salary. Salem Village had also separated from Salem Town seven years earlier. The people of the small farming village felt isolated from their richer, more powerful neighbors.

Strategy Tip

What does this illustration show you about how the Salem witch trials were conducted? Add this information to your KWL chart.

Puritans of Salem Village were eager to find something to blame for their recent troubles. Smallpox had killed many people in the 1680s and 1690s. Droughts in recent years had meant poor harvests. Those events had not happened by chance, people said; they were the result of witchcraft.

A witchcraft trial in Salem, Massachusetts, in 1692

Accused witches quickly filled the jail. A special court was created to deal with the witchcraft trials. Just a week after being established, the court convicted and hanged the first person accused of being a witch. One judge thought that relying only on the girls for evidence was wrong, so he resigned. Soon, he was accused of witchcraft, too.

Vocabulary Tip

This sentence says that with *spectral evidence,* "a person could be accused of causing harm with his or her spirit." What does that tell you about the meaning of *spectral*?

The court provided little help. The accused had no lawyers and were considered guilty unless proven innocent. Even more difficult to disprove was "**spectral evidence,**" which meant that a person could be accused of causing harm with his or her spirit. The accused person did not even need to be present because he or she was often already in jail.

History:
A Fever in the Land

Stories from the Trials

Each trial had its own horrors. The girls said the spirit of Sarah Goode's daughter, four-year-old Dorcas, had attacked them as revenge for accusing her mother. Encouraged by the judges, Dorcas told stories of the snake her mother had given her. She said her mother hurt the girls. Dorcas was clearly a witch, too. She joined her mother in jail. Then Sarah Goode was executed for witchcraft.

At first, Giles Corey, who was known for his temper, had believed in witches. He even accused his wife of witchcraft but then took back his testimony. The girls told the court how he had given them fits, pinched them, and plotted to destroy the church. The law said an accused person had three chances to plead. A person who did not answer could not be tried. Corey refused to speak, so the judges had him staked to the ground under a board. The judges ordered that the board be weighted with stones until Corey testified. He refused and was pressed to death.

One way to be accused of witchcraft was to be a member of the lower classes of Salem Village society. Another was to make fun of the girls. John Proctor, who criticized the girls and the trial process, became their target. He was, they said, "a most dreadful wizard." He, his wife, and their two oldest children were all accused. Despite his protests to officials in Boston, Proctor was hanged.

The Madness Slows

In October 1692, four months after the trials began, things began to change. The girls had accused the governor's wife and that went too far. Citizens from nearby communities wrote letters against the trials. Fourteen ministers finally urged an end to the trials. The Reverend Cotton Mather, who had been a believer in witchcraft, changed his mind. "I had rather judge a witch to be an honest woman than judge an honest woman to be a witch," he said.

When Mather wrote his protest, 150 suspected witches awaited trial. On October 15, the governor **disbanded** the court. When another court heard the cases, 49 of the 52 accused people were declared innocent. The other three confessed witches were later pardoned.

Twenty people had died, and a community had been torn apart. Finally, the accused returned to their homes. Several years passed before they regained their rights as citizens. In 1711, 22 relatives of those who had been executed asked for money to help pay for the loss of their family members. The court granted them their request.

Strategy Tip

Make sure your KWL notes are complete. The better your notes are, the easier it will be to write a summary.

Vocabulary Tip

Think about the meaning of the prefix *dis*—"the opposite of"—and you can understand the meaning of the word *disbanded.*

When you finish the article, complete the L column. Now look back at your W questions. Were they answered? You may want to reread the selection if you think the answers to your questions are in the article. When you finish, use your notes to write a summary of the article.

Apply It. . . . . To check your understanding of the selection, circle the best answer to each question below.

1. The main idea of this selection is that
   a. everyone in Salem was accused of witchcraft.
   b. no one was ever really punished for practicing witchcraft.
   c. anyone in Salem could be accused of witchcraft.
   d. innocent people were not convicted of witchcraft.

2. You can infer that one reason the girls talked of witchcraft was that
   a. they wanted to take revenge on people they disliked.
   b. they felt guilty about the forbidden games they had played.
   c. they wanted to please their parents.
   d. they wanted to see what would happen to the witches.

3. "As the women began to answer the questions, the girls again began writhing on the floor." In this sentence, the word *writhing* means
   a. wiggling.
   b. singing.
   c. pretending.
   d. crying.

4. Reverend Cotton Mather said, "I had rather judge a witch to be an honest woman than judge an honest woman to be a witch." What did he mean?
   a. He thought that protecting the guilty was more important than convicting the innocent.
   b. He thought protecting the innocent was more important than convicting the guilty.
   c. He wanted to force an end to the trials.
   d. He wanted to make sure that no witch escaped punishment.

5. It was not surprising that accusations of witchcraft were made in Salem Village because
   a. the people were not very religious.
   b. people felt isolated and tense about a number of issues.
   c. the children there had little to do.
   d. both b and c

Use the lines below to write your answers for numbers 6 and 7. Use your KWL chart to help you.

6. Why do you think the Salem witchcraft trials ended?

_____

_____

7. What lessons can people learn from the Salem witchcraft trials?

_____

_____

Test Tip

To answer question 7, think about how the witch trials in Salem are similar to and different from trials in the United States today.

Lesson 9 **63**

History:
Lesson 10   The Cruelest Journey

Hint

You can review the Cornell Note-taking strategy on page 8.

Understand It...... This history selection is about the Middle Passage, or the forced transportation of enslaved people from Africa to the Americas. Try the Cornell Note-taking strategy to help you remember the main ideas. This will help you focus on the main points of what you read.

Try It.............. Copy the Cornell chart below on another sheet of paper. Before you read, preview the article. Look at the title, the subheadings, and the map. The map shows the route ships took from Africa to the Americas. From that information and the title, you know you will be reading about the slave trade. Note any questions you have about the selection. After reading, remember to list the major points in the Main Points column of the chart and to list the supporting information in the Evidence/Details column. Then use your Cornell chart to write a summary of the selection.

Main Points	Evidence/Details

The Cruelest Journey

How did the enslavement of Africans in the Americas begin? The Spanish, who were the first explorers in the Americas, didn't plan it. Instead, they had planned to enslave Native Americans to do their work. The Spanish gave up that idea when the number of Native Americans quickly declined. Poor treatment by the Spaniards and European diseases killed thousands of Native Americans. The Spaniards needed to look elsewhere for labor. In 1501, the first enslaved Africans arrived in the Spanish colony of Hispaniola in the Caribbean. A 300-year trading system based on misery and enslavement had begun.

The Slave Trade Spreads
The slave trade soon spread to islands near Hispaniola. Enslaved people worked in Cuba, Puerto Rico, and Jamaica. The mainland colonies in what are now Mexico and Peru profited from enslaved people. From there, enslavement spread throughout South America.

The English began selling enslaved people in the Americas in the late 1500s. The French, the Dutch, and the Danes soon followed. Some North American colonists, watching the profits from enslavement go to Europeans, decided to get involved in the slave trade.

The first enslaved people in North America arrived in Jamestown, Virginia, in 1619. They were brought there by English slave traders. Enslavement spread throughout the colonies, particularly those in the South. In the latter part of the 17th century, the plantation system in the southern states required many more laborers than the plantation owners could afford to pay, which led to an increase in enslavement. About half a million people were captured in Africa and sent to North America before the African slave trade finally came to an end in 1808.

The slave trade from Africa became part of a three-sided trade route. Europe sent manufactured goods such as guns, iron, and textiles to Africa. Africa sent enslaved people to the Americas. Raw materials such as gold, sugar, silver, and tobacco traveled from the Americas to Europe. The enslaved people's trip from Africa to the Americas was called the Middle Passage because it was the middle section of the three-part journey.

Strategy Tip

When you read an article that contains a map, find places on the map as you read about them. Being able to see locations can help you remember geographic details.

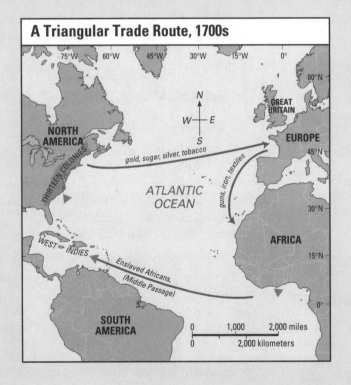

A Triangular Trade Route, 1700s

Enslavement

Africans became enslaved in several ways. Most, perhaps 80 percent, had lost wars. The victors sold them to slave traders. The more wars Africans fought among themselves, the more people were enslaved.

Other people were enslaved because they owed money and were sold to pay their debts. Occasionally, Africans convicted of crimes were sold into enslavement. **Infrequently**, individual Africans were kidnapped

Vocabulary Tip

You know the meaning of the word *frequently*. When the prefix *in-*, which means "not or no," is added, the word means "not frequently," or "not often."

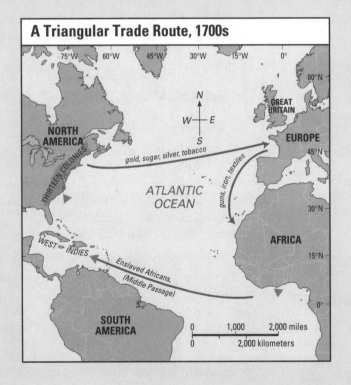

History:
The Cruelest Journey

and sold. Although enslavement through victory in war was common, individual kidnappings were not. Those who kidnapped ordinary people did so secretly. If discovered, they were likely to be severely punished by their own people because such kidnapping could lead to war.

Occasionally, African leaders tried to stop the slave trade. In the early 1500s, Afonso I, a ruler in west central Africa, became convinced that the Portuguese could bring improvements to his country, Kongo. The Portuguese did bring improvements. However, they brought the slave trade, too. Afonso protested that the traders were stealing the best young people the country had to offer, but no one listened. The slave trade was too profitable.

In 1788, the leader of Senegal declared that buyers could no longer transport enslaved people through his country. The business was too lucrative to stop. Before long, the slave traders had found another route to the coast.

Other African nations flourished through their involvement with the slave trade. The Ashanti kingdom, a coastal society north of Senegal, grew powerful and rich through enslavement. The royal family of the Ahsanti controlled trade, exchanging enslaved people for gold and guns.

The Dreaded Middle Passage

The horrors of the trip across the ocean are hard to grasp. A voyage took an average of two months. Enslaved Africans rarely had enough room to stand upright. They were chained together, ankle to ankle, and usually had about 3 feet in which to move. Some ships did not have enough room for everyone to lie down. People were forced to crouch in place. The temperature could be very hot. Occasionally, people were allowed on deck to stretch their legs. The slave ships were often called floating coffins. On a bad trip, as many as half the "passengers" died.

Gradually, conditions on slave ships improved. Traders saw they could make more money if they could keep more enslaved people alive during the trip. Shipbuilders provided portholes to circulate air. Captains kept some familiar foods in the Africans' diet, serving rice or yams along with the usual corn meal and palm oil mush.

One African died for every one who reached the Americas. Enslavement had an enormous impact on the generations that followed.

Strategy Tip
Test yourself by folding your Cornell chart so that you see only the main points. Can you list the supporting details for each one?

When you've finished creating your Cornell chart, look over what you have written. Your notes should contain the most important points and the details that explain them. When your notes are complete, use them to write a summary.

Apply It . . . . To check your understanding of the article, circle the best answer to each question below.

1. Which of these statements is true?
   a. Most enslaved Africans were sold because they were criminals.
   b. Most enslaved Africans were captured by Europeans.
   c. The American slave trade began when the Spanish wanted cheap labor.
   d. The American slave trade began when the Jamestown, Virginia, colonists bought enslaved people.

2. The term *Middle Passage* refers to
   a. the route from central Africa to the coast of Africa.
   b. the holds of the ships where enslaved people were kept.
   c. the passage of money between Europe and Africa.
   d. the journey of the slave ships from Africa to the Americas.

Test Tip

To answer question 3, substitute each choice for *lucrative*. Which word makes sense?

3. "The business was too lucrative to stop. Before long, the slave traders had found another route to the coast." In the passage, *lucrative* means
   a. profitable.
   b. unpopular.
   c. easy.
   d. inconvenient.

4. You can infer that the slave trade in the northern colonies of North America was not as strong because
   a. the economies of those colonies were less dependent on enslavement.
   b. the northern colonies were farther away from Africa.
   c. enslavement was outlawed in the northern colonies.
   d. enslavement was illegal in the southern colonies.

5. According to the article, conditions on slave ships improved because
   a. traders made more money if the enslaved people survived.
   b. traders began to see that enslavement was wrong.
   c. people in the Americas protested the poor conditions on the ships.
   d. ships were better designed and built.

Use the lines below to write your answers for numbers 6 and 7. Use your Cornell notes to help you.

6. Suppose you are Afonso I of Kongo. Write a letter or speech to Portugal protesting the slave trade.

   _____

   _____

7. Describe the journey an African might make from freedom in Africa to enslavement in the Americas.

   _____

   _____

Unit 3 Review
Reading in Social Studies

In this unit, you have practiced using the KWL Plus, Cornell Note-taking, PLAN, and DRTA strategies. Choose one strategy and use it when you read the selection below. Use a separate sheet of paper to draw charts, take notes, and summarize what you learn.

Hint *Remember that all reading strategies have activities for before, during, and after reading. To review these steps, look back at Unit 1 or at the last page of this book.*

Fall of the Berlin Wall

It was November 9, 1989. A man paused and then swung his hammer. Chunks of concrete came raining down. The crowd cheered. It was yet another blow at one of the most hated symbols in Europe: the Berlin Wall.

That night, the concrete and barbed-wire divider fell between East Berlin and West Berlin. A hated symbol of the Cold War after World War II became part of history.

The wall went up after Germany lost World War II. At the end of the war, Berlin was surrounded by the Soviets, who had fought on the side of the Allies against Germany. In 1949, the area officially became East Germany. As a result, Berlin was divided into East Berlin, which was controlled by the Soviets, and West Berlin, which was controlled by the French, British, and Americans.

Those in East Berlin soon realized that the economic conditions in their Communist part of the city were worse than the conditions in thriving West Berlin. East Germans began leaving for the West. In 1961, the wall went up to keep the East Germans from escaping to the capitalist West.

The wall was 12 feet high and 103 miles long, with deep ditches along the eastern side. There were two closely guarded openings in the wall, and East German soldiers patrolled them. The wall became a symbol of the tension between East and West and between communism and democracy. Yet, some people still managed to escape. More than 170 died, 59 as victims of bullets from East German guards.

In the late 1980s, communism began to fall apart in Eastern Europe. Hungary and Poland began economic programs that leaned away from communism. In the summer of 1989, the wall lost its power when Hungary began allowing East Germans to pass through Hungary on their way to nations such as West Germany.

Meanwhile, the East German government was on the edge of collapse. Soon citizens began taking down the wall. In 1990, the two

Germanys reunited as the Federal Republic of Germany.

While the joining of the two halves of Germany was significant, the more emotional event was the destruction of the wall. West Berliners threw flowers at their long-lost fellow residents. Families that had been separated reunited. Thousands streamed through the broken concrete. The cold war was over.

Use your notes and charts to help you answer the questions below.

1. Which is the best explanation of why the Berlin Wall was built?
    a. The Soviets built it to keep people from leaving Germany.
    b. East Germany built it to keep East Germans from leaving the country.
    c. East Germany built it to keep West Germany from attacking.
    d. West Germany built it to keep East Germans from coming to West Germany.

2. Which describes the correct order in which events occurred?
    a. Berlin was divided, the wall fell, East and West Germany reunited.
    b. The Berlin Wall was built, Berlin was divided into sectors, the two Berlins were reunited.
    c. The wall was built, the wall fell, many East Germans escaped into West Germany.
    d. East Germans escaped into West Germany, the two Germanys were reunited, the wall fell.

3. "While the joining of the two halves of Germany was significant, the more emotional event was the destruction of the wall." In this sentence, *significant* means
    a. easy.
    b. difficult.
    c. important.
    d. unimportant.

4. Explain why residents of East Germany felt safe destroying the wall in November of 1989.

_____

_____

5. Describe the effects of the Berlin Wall on the residents of East and West Berlin.

_____

_____

Unit 4
Reading in Science

You may read a newspaper article about a series of earthquakes or perhaps directions for assembling electronic equipment. When you do, you are using skills you need when you read science. The strategies you learn for reading science can help you in class and in everyday life.

How Science Reading Is Organized

Much of science reading is based on adding new information to what you already know. You learn about animals, and from there you learn about those that have backbones and those that do not. Because so much of science reading depends on basic knowledge, you shouldn't skip a word that you don't understand. That word may be important to your understanding of the whole selection.

Knowing the way the text is organized can also help you master science reading. When you recognize the pattern of the text, you can more easily fit the facts you learn into a larger picture. Here are some text patterns you may see in science reading.

Diagrams and Illustrations. In science readings, sometimes a diagram or illustration shows the main point of the reading. The text before and after the diagram or illustration explains it. You can better understand what the text is saying if you redraw the diagram and write an explanation of the concept.

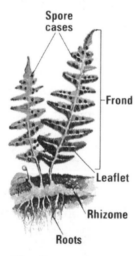

The Parts of a Fern

SCIENCE

Cause and Effect. Cause and effect is a common pattern in science reading. For example, a force such as wind may cause the effect of erosion. You may also read about causes and effects in relation to humans. Human actions may have effects on the earth and its inhabitants. When you see a cause-and-effect pattern, you may want to create a diagram like the one below to help you understand the reading.

Volcanic Eruption

| **Cause** Magma flows between rock layers of the crust through a fissure. | → | **Effect** (New Cause) Magma breaks through the crust. | → | **Effect** Magma, or lava, flows onto the surface of the earth. |

Main Idea and Details. This is a common pattern in reading about all subjects, including science. You will read about a main idea or ideas and the evidence or details that explain them. Science reading that discusses one topic may be organized this way. For example, a discussion of machines may include information on the six types. Below is an example of how this pattern might look.

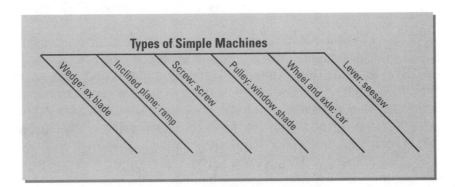

Types of Simple Machines

Wedge: ax blade

Inclined plane: ramp

Screw: screw

Pulley: window shade

Wheel and axle: car

Lever: seesaw

Getting the Most from Your Reading

When you recognize patterns of reading in science, you are better able to understand new information because you can think ahead to what you may be reading next. Making drawings like these may help you remember what is important about what you read.

Biology:

Lesson 11   The Case of the Abnormal Frogs

Understand It......

Hint
You can review the Cornell Note-taking strategy on page 8.

This selection is about a group of students who went on an ordinary field trip only to make some amazing discoveries. The observations they made had far-reaching effects, not only in their state but for the rest of the country.

Try It.............

The Cornell Note-taking strategy is a good one to use with this selection because it helps you focus on the selection's key ideas. Start by copying the chart shown below onto another sheet of paper. Before you read, preview the selection. Look at the subheadings, the first and last paragraphs, and the topic sentences to get an idea of what the author wants you to know. Fill in your chart after you read. Then use your Cornell chart to write a summary of the selection.

Strategy Tip

Include the words *frogs*, *abnormalities*, and *environment* in the Main Points column of your Cornell chart. In the Evidence/Details column, list details that support or explain the main points you find.

Main Points	Evidence/Details

Vocabulary Tip

The word *abnormal* is an adjective that means "not normal, or unusual." A related noun is *abnormalities*. What do you think *abnormalities* means?

The Case of the Abnormal Frogs

In August of 1995, a high-school nature studies class went on a field trip. The students hiked through a wildlife game refuge near Henderson, Minnesota. They observed their surroundings and took notes. In one area, the group discovered a large population of frogs. When the students examined the frogs, they were shocked. Many of the frogs were deformed. Most of the deformities involved the legs. Many frogs had one abnormal leg and one healthy leg. Some frogs had only one leg. Others had an extra leg. The students also found **abnormalities** in other body parts, especially the eyes.

The students collected data on the number of frogs observed and the number of abnormalities present. Then they analyzed their data. They found that about half of their specimens had a physical abnormality.

Back at school, the students wondered what might have caused the abnormalities. They began conducting research. They contacted local farmers to ask what kinds of chemicals they used. The class posted pictures of the deformed frogs on the Internet. The students reported their findings to the Minnesota Pollution Control Agency.

A local newspaper ran the story. One week later, a television station reported the discovery on an evening news program. Two weeks later, the Associated Press picked up the story. Newspapers and radio and television stations from around the country wanted information.

A deformed Northern Leopard Frog

Scientists from around the state—and around the country—became interested. They thought the abnormal frogs might be related to a trend already noted by many professionals. Frog populations are shrinking worldwide. Certain species of frogs have fewer members than they did a decade ago. Other species no longer live in areas they once did. Some species have completely disappeared.

Many researchers suspect that the disappearing frogs signal problems in the environment. Scientists know that frogs are very sensitive to pollution. Because they live in places where land and water meet, they are affected by pollutants from the land and the water. Scientists worry that habitat changes cause changes in the frogs.

The Minnesota Pollution Control Agency has conducted many tests on the deformed frogs' environment. Early results show that the abnormalities might be caused by something in the water. However, the researchers haven't identified what that might be. The agency has also conducted tests to determine whether the unknown agent might harm humans living in the region.

Today the agency works with other agencies throughout the country. The researchers hope to find the cause of the changes in frog populations. By pooling their findings, the agencies hope to solve the case of the abnormal frogs.

When you finish reading, use your Cornell notes to write a summary of the selection. The summary should include the important points and details to back them up.

Apply It............ To check your understanding of the selection, circle the best answer to each question below.

1. What did the students find in the wildlife refuge?
   a. a large number of abnormal frogs
   b. that the water was polluted
   c. many kinds of animals with abnormalities
   d. that there were fewer frogs than they expected

Biology:
The Case of the Abnormal Frogs

Test Tip

Question 2 tests your ability to define a word in the second paragraph. Look for clues in the paragraph to understand the meaning of *specimens*.

2. In the second paragraph, *specimens* means
   a. any type of frog or toad.
   b. organisms that live outdoors.
   c. objects being studied.
   d. imperfect items.

3. What did the students do immediately after finding the frogs?
   a. They took notes on their findings.
   b. They contacted local television stations.
   c. They posted pictures on the Internet.
   d. They spoke to the Minnesota Pollution Control Agency.

4. Scientist know that frogs are very sensitive to
   a. changes in temperature.
   b. handling by humans.
   c. radiation.
   d. pollution.

5. Scientists think that a substance in the water in the frogs' environment
   a. definitely harms humans.
   b. harms frogs.
   c. doesn't harm all living things.
   d. helps the frogs reproduce.

Use the lines below to write your answers for numbers 6 and 7. Use your Cornell notes and summary to help you.

6. Write a paragraph describing what the Minnesota class found.

_____

_____

_____

_____

7. Suppose you could interview one of the students on the field trip. Make a list of three questions you would ask the student.

_____

_____

_____

Lesson 12

Technology: Spin-Offs from Space

Hint
You can review the PLAN strategy on page 12.

Understand It...... Do you think space exploration has any effect on your everyday life? You probably don't—unless you are an astronaut. However, many products you use every day are the result of space exploration. In this selection, you will learn about how space technology benefits people on Earth.

Try It............. Use the PLAN strategy to understand the relationship between space science and household products. Begin by copying one of the PLAN word maps onto another sheet of paper. A wheel-and-spoke diagram might work well because the article focuses on one topic: how space technologies led to new products for everyday use. However, use the graphic that works best for you.

Strategy Tip
When making your predictions, consider what you already know about space exploration and technology.

First, predict the kind of information you might read in the article. You can make predictions by previewing the article. Record your predictions in the word map. Next, locate important information. Write check marks next to points you know about and question marks next to points you don't know about.

After you read the selection, add words that will help you remember this information. Later, note what you have learned by summarizing the article.

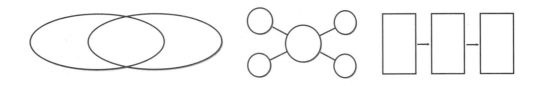

Vocabulary Tip
The adjective *spin-off* is used often today. TV characters move from one series to a new one. This is called a *spin-off* series. What might a *spin-off product* be?

Spin-Offs from Space

The exploration of space began in 1957. In that year, the Soviet Union launched a satellite called Sputnik. Since then, hundreds of artificial satellites have orbited Earth. Many have gathered information about our solar system.

Spacecraft, space probes, and space stations followed satellites into space. The aerospace industry needed the most up-to-date technologies to build these vehicles. Developing the new technologies requires thousands of experiments. However, when the work is done, the knowledge can be used in a variety of ways. The technology that sends people into space can also be used to make everyday products. A **spin-off product** results from the development of an unrelated product.

Small radios, computers, and televisions were originally products made for space travel. Space travel is very expensive. Using smaller, lighter equipment saves money.

Technology:
Spin-Offs from Space

Strategy Tip

Reading the topic
sentences of every
paragraph will show you
the variety of spin-off
products that have been
developed. Add these
products to your PLAN
graphic.

Non-stick cookware is another spin-off. The coating on the cookware was first used on the outside of spacecraft. Scientists realized that a form of the coating would keep food from sticking to cookware. They applied aerospace technology to something people use every day. The result was non-stick cookware.

People who wear glasses got some help. Scientists needed to reduce surface friction on spacecraft. They knew that smooth objects produce less friction than rough objects. They needed to find a way to keep a spacecraft's surface smooth. The scientists also knew that diamonds are very hard. They hypothesized that covering a craft's surface with a diamondlike substance would prevent scratching. They figured that keeping the craft smooth would reduce surface friction. Many experiments proved the hypothesis correct. Scientists were able to apply their knowledge to an everyday product. The lenses of glasses have a similar coating. The coating makes the lenses ten times more resistant to scratches than lenses without it.

Aerospace technology also introduced new ways of using spin-off products at home. For example, freeze-dried foods are lighter and last longer. Now people can buy some freeze-dried foods in supermarkets.

Even babies can use spin-offs. In the early 1980s, scientists thought algae might be a good food for astronauts. The scientists identified the nutrients in algae. Human milk also contains some of those nutrients. The nutrients help babies develop mentally. However, most baby formulas lack those nutrients. A spin-off product was soon developed. Parents can mix an additive containing the nutrients with their baby's formula. In this case, the spin-off just might be more important than the original!

Now that you have finished reading the selection, complete your PLAN graphic. When you are satisfied that you've included all the important information, note what you have learned. Review it in your mind or redraw your map if that would help you.

To check your understanding of the selection, circle the best answer to each question below.

Apply It. . . . . To check your understanding of the selection, circle the best answer to each question below.

1. The main idea of this selection is that
   a. only astronauts benefit from space exploration.
   b. new products are always being developed.
   c. the exploration of space is a relatively new field.
   d. some space technology can be adapted to make everyday products.

2. A spin-off product is
   a. an item that results from the development of an unrelated product.
   b. an item that continuously moves in a circle.
   c. an item that is created in a scientific laboratory.
   d. an item made in the aerospace industry.

3. Scientists applied information about the outer covering of spacecraft to
   a. the development of radios.
   b. baby formula.
   c. cookware.
   d. making fruit snacks.

Test Tip

To *hypothesize* means "to guess about what is most likely to happen." A hypothesis is based on known facts. To answer question 4, think about a fact that scientists used to form their hypothesis.

4. Why did scientists hypothesize that they should cover the surface of a spacecraft with a diamondlike substance?
   a. They thought the diamondlike substance would reduce scratching.
   b. They thought smooth objects encounter less friction than rough objects.
   c. They thought friction acts on diamonds.
   d. both a and b

5. According to the selection, algae and human milk are alike in that both
   a. are produced through technology.
   b. are needed by developing infants.
   c. contain some of the same nutrients.
   d. can be used as a food source on space missions.

Use the lines below to write your answers for numbers 6 and 7. Use your PLAN notes to help you.

6. Choose one product mentioned in this article. Describe how space technology was used to improve it.

_____

_____

_____

7. Do you think the benefits of space science are worth the cost? Express your thoughts in a paragraph.

_____

_____

_____

_____

_____

Health Science:
Lesson 13 Steroid Use Among Athletes

Understand It......

Hint
You can review the KWL Plus strategy on page 4.

Do you work out? Thousands of people do. People work hard to build strong, fit bodies. In this selection, you will learn about other things people do to increase their physical strength. You've probably heard something about the use and abuse of steroids. KWL Plus is a good reading strategy to use when you know something about the subject.

Try It..............

Copy the KWL chart shown below onto another piece of paper. List everything you know about steroid use among athletes in the K column. In the W column, write what you want to know about steroid use. Write the answers to your questions in the L column after you read. Then use your KWL chart to write a summary of the selection.

Strategy Tip

Before you begin writing what you know, preview the selection. Previewing will help you see what the author's main points will be. This will help you ask questions that the selection will answer.

K (What I know)	W (What I want to know)	L (What I've learned)

Vocabulary Tip

The word *cortical* means "of or related to" the *cortex*. The cortex is the outer layer of the brain. *Cortical* is an adjective that means "connected to the action of the cortex."

Steroid Use Among Athletes

If you enjoy sports, you've probably heard the term *steroids*. Steroids are a group of compounds found in nature. The human body naturally produces two kinds of steroids. One kind of steroid is called **cortical** steroids. Cortical steroids are made by the adrenal glands. The adrenal glands are located at the top of the kidneys.

Drug companies make many different kinds of cortical steroids. Artificial steroids are just like the ones the body makes. Doctors use artificial steroids to treat different conditions, such as allergies, asthma, and certain skin disorders.

Cortisone is a very popular cortical steroid. It is used to treat people who suffer from arthritis. Cortisone reduces the pain caused by inflamed and swollen joints. That helps patients move about more easily.

Human reproductive organs naturally produce other kinds of steroids. Anabolic steroids are drugs similar to the steroid produced by males. These drugs stimulate muscle growth and tissue repair.

Many athletes take anabolic steroids to increase their strength and endurance. They believe that the drugs help them perform better. However, many sports organizations have banned the use of anabolic steroids. In 1975, the International Olympic Committee outlawed the use of steroids. The committee thought that athletes who use steroids have an unfair advantage over athletes who don't use drugs.

SCIENCE

Charts are often used in science texts to give more specific information about a topic. What does this chart tell you about steroids?

Differences between Cortical and Anabolic Steroids

TYPE	EFFECTS
Cortical	reduces the pain caused by inflamed and swollen joints; also helps people who have allergies, asthma, and certain skin disorders
Anabolic	natural amounts: increase strength and endurance overuse: stunts growth; creates heart and liver disease and sterility; increases aggression

In that same year, Olympic officials began testing athletes for drug use. Since then, a number of Olympic athletes have tested positive and have been stripped of their medals. In 1988, Canadian sprinter Ben Johnson lost his gold medal after testing positive for steroid use. Johnson was also banned from competition for two years. Four years later, he ran in the Olympic Games again. One year later, he tested positive for steroid use and was again banned from competition.

Using anabolic steroids can do much more than cause an athlete to lose a gold medal. Prolonged use of the drugs have severe effects on the user's body. Heart disease, liver disease, sterility, and increased aggression are some known side effects in adult users.

Use of steroids during the teenage years can stunt the user's growth, in addition to causing the same side effects noted in adults. However, studies show that steroid use has increased among teens since the 1980s. That is especially true among young women. Researchers believe that the recent focus on women's sports has contributed to the rise in the number of female athletes who use steroids.

If anabolic steroids pose a health risk, why would any athlete take them? Many people believe the drugs give them a competitive edge. For high-school athletes, being a winner might mean a chance at a college scholarship. However, users forget one very important fact. As the drug builds up one area of the body, it destroys another area. So steroids may help an athlete increase his or her performance now, but they will also seriously affect the person's health in the future.

Now that you have finished reading the selection, complete the L column of your chart. Include facts you hadn't asked questions about, too. When you are satisfied with your chart, use it to write a summary of the information you learned when you read.

Health Science:
Steroid Use Among Athletes

Apply It. . . . . To check your understanding of the selection, circle the best answer to each question below.

1. The adrenal glands are located
   a. at the top of the kidneys.
   b. in the male reproductive system.
   c. in the muscular system.
   d. in tissue throughout the body.

Test Tip

In question 2, the word *except* tells you that three of the choices *are* treated by cortical steroids. You are looking for the one that is not.

2. All of the following can be treated with cortical steroids except
   a. asthma.
   b. allergies.
   c. heart disease.
   d. skin disorders.

3. Athletes take anabolic steroids to
   a. increase strength and endurance.
   b. develop bone and ligaments.
   c. strengthen the circulatory system.
   d. lose weight.

4. Why did the International Olympic Committee ban anabolic steroids?
   a. Not every participant could afford the drug.
   b. Committee members thought steroid users had an unfair advantage.
   c. People who do not use steroids are healthier.
   d. Steroids are available only in the United States.

5. Why is steroid use particularly dangerous to teens?
   a. Steroids cannot be obtained legally.
   b. Steroids cause swelling in the joints.
   c. Steroids cause loss of memory.
   d. Steroids can stunt growth.

Use the lines below to write your answers for numbers 6 and 7. Use your KWL chart to help you.

6. Write a few sentences for a youth sports organization in your community that explains the dangers of steroid use.

_____

_____

_____

7. Suppose you were a high-school athlete encouraged to take anabolic steroids by your teammates. How would you respond?

_____

_____

Lesson 14

Chemistry: Chemical Weapons

Understand It......

Hint

You can review the PLAN strategy on page 12.

Technology provides people with new ways of doing work or having fun. Most of those discoveries make life better in one way or another. Unfortunately, certain technological advances have had harmful effects on humans. In this selection, you will learn about these terrifying weapons made by technology. Try the PLAN strategy to help you understand the main points of this selection.

Try It..............

Start by previewing the reading. When you preview, you'll notice some dates. Maybe the reading is organized in chronological, or time, order. If it is, the sequence chart might be the best choice.

Draw the word map you choose on another sheet of paper. Then predict the kind of information you will read in the article. Record your predictions in your word map. Then locate important information. Write check marks next to information you know about. Write question marks next to information you don't know about. After you read, add words to your word map that will help you remember this information. When you have finished reading, summarize what you have learned.

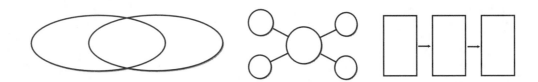

Strategy Tip

The title identifies the topic of the selection. Use what you learn when you preview to make some predictions about the topic.

Chemical Weapons

Our world is quite different from the world of our grandparents and great-grandparents. Technology has given humans cars, television, and computers. They all help make daily life a bit easier or more enjoyable.

Although most technological developments have positive effects, there are some exceptions. The creation of chemical weapons for battle is one example. Chemical weapons are chemical substances that disable or kill humans.

The first known use of chemical weapons occurred more than 70 years ago. In World War I, the German army used two types of chemical weapons. In 1915, German soldiers placed containers holding liquid chlorine along a battlefield. When French troops entered the area, the Germans fired at the containers. The bullets shattered the containers. Deadly gas spread over the battlefield. The chemical weapon claimed the lives of more than 5,000 French soldiers in a single afternoon, and the gas injured more than 10,000 others.

Chemistry:
Chemical Weapons

Later in the war, the Germans used mustard gas. That gas was deadlier than liquid chlorine. Artillery shells carried mustard gas to its victims. As the shells exploded, the gas escaped. Unsuspecting soldiers suddenly smelled an odd odor. Then they began to vomit. Their eyes burned and their vision blurred. Huge blisters appeared on their bodies. When the gas reached their respiratory system, breathing became difficult. Eventually, their respiratory systems shut down, and many died.

Some experts believe chemical weapons killed more than 100,000 soldiers during World War I. Chemical weapons caused nearly 30 percent of all U.S. casualties.

After the war ended, world leaders took steps to stop the use of the deadly weapons. In 1925, a treaty limiting the use of chemical weapons was introduced. More than 100 countries signed the treaty. Each promised not to use such weapons except in **retaliation**.

In spite of the treaty, mustard gas has found its way back into modern warfare. During the 1980s, Iraq and Iran went to war. Evidence shows that the Iraqis used mustard gas against their Iranian enemies. Some experts also believe that the Iraqis used chemical weapons during the Persian Gulf War in 1991.

More than 20 countries have chemical weapons available for use. Those countries are not breaking the 1925 treaty. Signers of that treaty agreed not to *use* chemical weapons. They didn't promise not to produce them. Perhaps the time has come for world leaders to rewrite the original treaty. A new treaty might end the production of these agents of destruction.

Soldiers practicing for a chemical weapon attack

Vocabulary Tip

The noun *retaliation* means "the act of returning an evil for an evil." The verb form of the word is *retaliate*.

Strategy Tip

What does this photo tell you about how chemical weapons work? Add this information to your PLAN word map.

After you finish reading the selection, complete your PLAN graphic. When you are satisfied that your word map is complete, note what you have learned. You can review the information by summarizing the selection.

Apply It. . . . . To check your understanding of the selection, circle the best answer to each question below.

1. Chemical weapons
    a. kill living things.
    b. injure living things.
    c. make living things stronger.
    d. both a and b

2. Liquid chlorine can be used to
    a. create a deadly gas.
    b. make mustard gas.
    c. explode artillery shells.
    d. both a and b

3. Mustard gas kills by damaging its victims'
    a. digestive systems.
    b. circulatory systems.
    c. respiratory systems.
    d. reproductive systems.

4. The 1925 treaty doesn't ban
    a. the use of chemical weapons in battle.
    b. the production of chemical weapons.
    c. sharing supplies of chemical weapons.
    d. either a or b

Test Tip

To correctly answer question 5, reread the last two sentences of the selection. Do they state something that can be proven? Do they state a wish the author has?

5. The last two sentences of the selection state
    a. an opinion.
    b. a fact.
    c. information used to amuse the reader.
    d. research on the topic.

Use the lines below to write your answers for numbers 6 and 7. Use your PLAN notes to help you.

6. Write a persuasive letter to an elected official urging the creation of a new chemical weapons treaty. Use facts to support your stand.

    _____

    _____

    _____

    _____

7. Why do you think nations want to ban only chemical weapons, not traditional weapons?

    _____

    _____

    _____

    _____

Genetics: Cloning

Understand It......

Have you ever wondered where the food you eat comes from? Few people have. Most people simply buy what they need at a grocery store. They don't have to worry about growing their own food. That's a farmer's job. In this selection, you will discover that it is also a scientist's job. Because you may not know much about cloning, the Cornell Note-taking strategy is a good one to use. It can help you understand the key ideas of a selection.

Try It...............

Copy the chart shown below. Remember to preview before you read. You want to get an idea of what the author is going to tell you. That will help you focus on the selection's main points.

Strategy Tip
The words *cloning* and *controlled breeding* should be included in the Main Points column of your Cornell chart. In the Evidence/Details column, list details that support or explain those key words.

Main Points	Evidence/Details

Cloning

Animals and plants are bred so they will have traits that people want. Dogs are bred to do certain jobs, such as herding sheep. Plants such as wheat and corn are bred to produce nutritious food crops.

Early people did not have modern technology to help them produce healthy organisms. However, they did know that if they planted seeds from productive plants, they could grow more of the same kinds of plants. Early farmers also knew that the offspring of strong animals had the same traits as their parents. They mated animals with **desirable** traits to produce more animals with the same traits.

Vocabulary Tip
The word *desirable* means "pleasing or wanted." A synonym for *desirable* is *favorable*.

The process of carefully breeding organisms with certain traits is called controlled breeding. Although early humans practiced controlled breeding, they had no idea why it worked.

Today, scientists know how parents pass traits to offspring. Genes control the traits of an organism. Genes are units of hereditary information. Offspring receive genes from each parent. Those genes are copies of the parents' genes. That is why offspring generally have the same traits as their parents.

Cloning in Plants

Vocabulary Tip
Use the information in this paragraph to define *cloning*.

Recently, scientists have found a way to produce an organism that has exactly the same genes as one parent. The process is called **cloning**. You might have actually "cloned" a plant yourself. Have you ever taken a cutting from a plant to grow a new plant? If so, you probably put the cutting into water. After a time, the cutting developed roots. If you planted the rooted cutting, a new plant grew. The new plant was identical to the "parent." The new plant had the same genes as the original plant.

Cloning has made new types of fruit available. One is the seedless orange. A few years ago, an orange grower noticed that the fruit of one orange tree lacked seeds. That change in the oranges had happened naturally. The orange grower also discovered that the seedless oranges were juicier and sweeter than ordinary oranges. The grower took a branch from the seedless orange tree and attached it to the trunk of an ordinary orange tree. The branch continued to produce seedless oranges. Over time, more and more branches from the ordinary tree also began producing seedless oranges. Through cloning, thousand of seedless orange trees exist today.

Cloning in Animals

However, the most startling use of cloning to date occurred in 1996. Scottish scientists cloned an adult sheep. The clone, called Dolly, is identical to her six-year-old parent. Many people hailed the breakthrough as one of the greatest scientific acts of the past 50 years. However, people also worry about cloning. They feel that it is only a matter of time before scientists try to clone humans. Many believe cloning humans would be overstepping the line of scientific research.

Dolly, the cloned sheep

Strategy Tip

The subheadings show you that the article discusses two different types of cloning: cloning in plants and cloning in animals. Include both types of cloning in your Cornell chart.

Now use your Cornell notes to write a summary of the selection. The summary should include the important points and details to back them up.

Apply It. . . . . To check your understanding of the selection, circle the best answer to each question below.

1. Genes can be described as
   a. traits of plants.
   b. types of breeding methods.
   c. cuttings.
   d. units of hereditary information.

Genetics: Cloning

Test Tip

The word *alike* in question 2 shows that you must name a similarity between cloning and controlled breeding. The correct answer must describe *both* processes.

2. How are cloning and controlled breeding alike?
   a. Both processes produce parents.
   b. Both were used by farmers hundreds of years ago.
   c. Both produce offspring with desirable traits.
   d. Both produce genes.

3. What caused the first seedless orange tree?
   a. a change that occurred naturally
   b. controlled breeding
   c. cloning
   d. a new type of seed

4. The selection says that cloning
   a. can be used only to create identical copies of plants.
   b. can be used to create identical copies of plants and animals.
   c. was used hundreds of years ago by farmers.
   d. makes Scottish scientists more advanced than U.S. scientists.

5. Who was Dolly?
   a. She was the first scientist who produced a cloned organism.
   b. She was the first cloned sheep.
   c. She was an orange grower who discovered seedless oranges.
   d. She is the author of this selection.

Use the lines below to write your answers for numbers 6 and 7. Use your Cornell notes and summary to help you.

6. Explain how a breeder could use controlled breeding to develop a new kind of plant or animal.

   _____

   _____

   _____

   _____

7. Do you think scientists should continue to clone plants and animals? Why or why not?

   _____

   _____

   _____

   _____

Lesson 16

Lab Activity: Water Loss in Plants

Understand It...... Living and nonliving things interact with one another and with their physical environment. Those interactions help organisms obtain the materials they need to carry out their life processes. This selection gives directions for a lab activity that explores how a plant process provides people with a substance they need to live—water.

Hint
You can review the DRTA strategy on page 16.

Try It.............. DRTA is a good strategy to use with this reading because you probably know something about the relationship between plants and water. This knowledge will make it easy for you to make predictions after you preview the reading. You know you're going to follow the steps of a procedure, make some observations, and draw some conclusions.

Start by copying the DRTA chart below onto a sheet of paper. Then preview the selection. Make some predictions about what you will learn by reading the activity. Record your predictions in the Preview box on your chart, then read the selection. After you read, look for evidence that supports your predictions and write it in the Take Notes box. Finally, write a summary in the Review box.

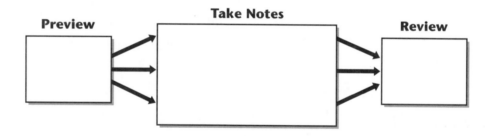

Strategy Tip
Carefully read the subheadings in the lab activity. After you preview, try to make one prediction about what you will learn in each section.

Water Loss in Plants

Background Information
    Water that falls on land may be absorbed from the soil by plants. Some of that water evaporates from the leaves of plants and returns to the air. Plants may use the rest of the water to make food through photosynthesis. Some of the water in the plants passes to animals that eat the plants. That water plus the water the animals drink is released into the air when the animals exhale water vapor.

Materials
3 geranium leaves with stems attached	cardboard
6 pint jars	scissors
large box	labels
petroleum jelly	water

Lab Activity:
Water Loss in Plants

Procedure

1. Cut three pieces of cardboard. Each piece should be large enough to completely cover the top of a jar. Poke a small hole in the center of each cardboard piece.

2. Insert the stem of one leaf through the hole in one piece of cardboard. Plug the hole with petroleum jelly.

3. Pour water into the jar until it is half full. Place the cardboard with the inserted stem on top of the jar. The stem should hang down into the water.

4. Turn another jar upside down and put it on top of the cardboard so that it encloses the leaf. Label the jar *Light*. Put the set-up in a sunny place.

5. Repeat Steps 1 through 4 with another leaf, cardboard piece, and jars. Label that jar *Dark*. Cover the set-up with a large box that will keep out the light.

6. Coat the third leaf with a thick layer of petroleum jelly. Repeat Steps 1 through 4 with the coated leaf. Label the jar *Control*. Place that set-up alongside the *Light* set-up.

   After a few hours, look at the jars on the top of each set-up. Record your observations.

Observations

1. What did you **observe** in each jar?

2. Where did the water come from? What evidence do you have to support your idea?

3. What was the purpose of the set-up labeled *Control*?

4. Which top jar contained the greatest amount of water?

Conclusions

1. Do plants lose more water during the day or at night? Support your response with evidence from the lab activity.

2. Use what you observed to explain how plants contribute to the water cycle.

Vocabulary Tip

The word *observe* is a verb that means "to see or watch." Two related nouns are *observation,* which is "something that is observed," and *observatory,* which is "a place for making observations."

Now complete the Take Notes section of your DRTA chart with the main points of the reading. Use your notes to write a few sentences in the Review section that summarize the main points. If possible, carry out the experiment to check your predictions and your understanding of the activity.

SCIENCE

Apply It............ To check your understanding of the selection, circle the best answer to each question below.

1. What type of information is provided in the Materials section?
   a. a list of the items needed for the activity
   b. questions to be answered through the activity
   c. additional information about the activity topic
   d. steps to follow when carrying out the activity

2. Read through the Procedure section before beginning the activity to
   a. make sure the necessary supplies are available.
   b. discover the purpose of the activity.
   c. draw a conclusion about the activity.
   d. make sure you understand the steps of the process.

3. According to the Procedure section, what must be done immediately after a stem is inserted through a cardboard hole?
   a. Fill each jar with water.
   b. Plug the hole with petroleum jelly.
   c. Place a jar over the leaf.
   d. Put the stem in a dark place.

Test Tip

The correct response to question 4 calls for an inference. Ask yourself why the procedure calls for placing the set-ups in different locations. What variable changes? The answers will lead you to the correct inference.

4. What can you infer from the fact that one set-up is placed in a sunny location while another set-up is covered with a box?
   a. The amount of oxygen available will affect the results.
   b. Sunlight has no effect on the process being investigated.
   c. Results will differ in sunlight and in darkness.
   d. Most labs have few sunny locations.

5. The purpose of the activity is to
   a. explore how plants contribute to the water cycle.
   b. compare daylight and darkness.
   c. discover how water helps plants grow.
   d. see how lack of oxygen affects plant growth.

Use the lines below to write your answers for numbers 6 and 7. Use your DRTA chart to help you.

6. Suppose the stems were placed in empty jars. Do you think the results would be different? Explain.

   _____

   _____

7. Predict the type of problems that might arise if a student used only two stems: one in the light set-up and the other as the control.

   _____

   _____

Unit 4 Review
Reading in Science

In this unit, you have practiced using the KWL Plus, Cornell Note-taking, PLAN, and DRTA strategies. Choose one strategy and use it when you read the selection below. Use a separate sheet of paper to draw charts, take notes, and summarize what you learn.

Hint *Remember that all reading strategies have activities for before, during, and after reading. To review these steps, look back at Unit 1 or at the last page of this book.*

Get that Lollipop Out of Your Mouth

Every schoolchild has heard it: Don't eat so much sugar; it will ruin your teeth. Do the parents who say this know what they're talking about? It seems they do.

Even the ancient Greeks had a suspicion that there was a relationship between sugar and the destruction of teeth. Aristotle wrote, "Why do figs, which are soft and sweet, destroy the teeth?"

About 2,000 years later, in the 1500s, upper-class Europeans suddenly had an alarming increase in cavities. That increase happened when pure sugar from the West Indies sugarcane plantations became available. It wasn't long before the connection was common knowledge, but no one knew the exact reason until the 20th century.

Researchers found that certain types of *Streptococcus* bacteria find sugar a wonderful medium in which to thrive. Those bacteria form acids that eat away at the enamel of teeth. As the enamel breaks down, other bacteria enter the tooth. Before long, these bacteria eat holes in the teeth and cause a cavity, or hole.

If nothing is done to stop the process, decay can cause infection deep in the tooth. If that goes untreated, the jawbone may be affected. When the tooth is this damaged by decay, about the only avenue is root-canal therapy. In this procedure, the dentist digs deep into the root of the tooth to remove the infected material. When all else fails, the dentist must remove the tooth.

Today, dentists deal with cavities by removing the decayed part of the tooth and replacing it with a material such as gold, a silver compound, porcelain, or plastic.

In 1949, researchers proved that a small amount of sodium fluoride reduced cavities. Since then, fluoride has been added to most drinking water in the United States. As a result, there has been less tooth decay.

The greatest factor in creating cavities is the length of time sugar is in contact with the bacteria that lives on teeth. For example, eating small, frequent snacks is more harmful than a sugar-eating binge. Also, candies that are sucked, like lollipops, or that stick to the teeth, like caramels, are more harmful than candies that are quickly eaten. Carbohydrates such as potato chips can be a problem, too, because they are broken down into sugars by saliva.

If this brief tour of tooth decay has you concerned about keeping your teeth cavity-free, here is another tip. A few foods—some cheeses and teas—seem to slow the growth of bacteria. Although no one knows why, there may be traces of antibiotics in these foods that keeps bacteria at bay. In the meantime, keep your toothbrush handy.

Use your notes to help you answer the questions below.

1. According to the article, which of these statements is true?
   a. Sugar causes cavities.
   b. Bacteria cause cavities.
   c. Carbohydrates stop cavities from forming.
   d. both a and b

2. Which of the following seem to prevent bacteria from forming?
   a. some teas
   b. potato chips
   c. some cheeses
   d. a and c

3. Why do carbohydrates help cause tooth decay?
   a. They are able to get into the plaque and create cavities.
   b. They are broken down into acid that causes tooth decay.
   c. They are broken down into sugars by saliva.
   d. Carbohydrates do not cause tooth decay.

4. Why was tooth decay an upper-class disease in Europe in the 1500s?

   _____

   _____

5. Describe the process by which a dentist may deal with tooth decay.

   _____

   _____

Unit 5
Reading in Mathematics

Mathematics isn't just equations and numbers. It is also words that explain those equations. You read math whenever you analyze an ad to see how much money you will save in a sale. You use math when you double a recipe, or look at the win–loss record of your favorite team. Feeling confident when you are reading mathematics can help you in daily life.

How Mathematics Reading Is Organized

Reading mathematics is not like reading literature. For example, when you are reading a play, you might be able to skip a word you do not know and still get the general idea of the reading. In math, you must pay attention to each word, as well as the symbols, numbers, and equations you see. The more you pay attention to them, the better your understanding will be. Much of mathematics builds on what you already know. If you read carefully and notice the patterns in math reading, you will be better able to understand what you read.

Main Idea and Details. Some mathematics reading is descriptive. It may explain a theory or describe the life of a famous mathematician. When you see this pattern, you will often see several main points connected to the topic. Below is an example of how this structure might look in a graphic:

Steps of a Process. Often in math you will read to understand a process. You may read to find the steps for converting decimals to percentages or for converting temperature scales. When you see this pattern, look for the next step. Here are two ways of getting the most out of this kind of reading. First, rewrite the steps in your own words. Second, try several examples to make sure you understand the process. Here is an example of how this pattern may look:

Multiplying Fractions

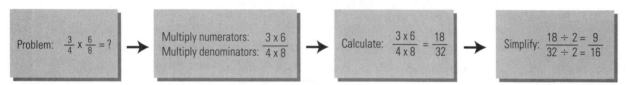

Text and Symbols. When you read mathematics, look at the symbols as if they were words. A sentence in math may be composed of just symbols. One way to do this is to write out the meaning of the equation. Here is an example:

Area of a Triangle

$A = \frac{1}{2} \times b \times h$

Area equals $\frac{1}{2}$ times *base* times *height*

Getting the Most from Your Reading

If you can recognize patterns in reading math texts, you will be better prepared to learn new information. Making diagrams, rewriting steps in your own words, and trying out example problems are good ways of understanding math readings.

Real-life Math:
Lesson 17   Balancing a Checking Account

Understand It......

Hint
You can review the KWL Plus strategy on page 4.

In this selection, you will learn how to balance a checking account. Understanding this information will help you develop a skill that you will use often in your adult life.

You may know something about checking accounts. Maybe you have your own savings account. Try the KWL Plus strategy with this reading. It works well when you already know something about the topic.

Try It..............

Copy the KWL chart onto another piece of paper. Then list everything you know about checking accounts in the K column. Next, preview the reading, looking for numbers and unfamiliar words. In the W column, write what you want to know about checking accounts. When you finish reading, you will write what you have learned in the L column. Then you will use your KWL chart to summarize the selection.

Strategy Tip
When you think about what you know about checking accounts, think about how and why people use them.

K (What I know)	W (What I want to know)	L (What I've learned)

Balancing a Checking Account

Think about all the things adults have to pay for. Rent, insurance, groceries, telephone bills—the list goes on. Because sending cash isn't a good idea, most people use checks, which people can exchange for money.

You can open a checking account at almost any bank. You make an initial, or first, deposit. After you make your deposit, you can write checks on that money. You must record *every* check written in your record book. You note the check number, the date, the person who will receive it, and the amount. Then you deduct the amount of the check from the total. The remainder is the amount of money left in your account.

Your Bank Statement
Once a month, the bank will send you a statement. Your statement lists all the deposits you made during the month. It also lists all the checks that the bank has paid from your account during the month. These are your canceled checks. When you get your monthly statement, you'll want to **balance** your checkbook.

Balancing your checkbook means making sure the amount of money you have in your account is correct. If you have kept careful records of every deposit and every check, then balancing your account will be easy.

Vocabulary Tip
Notice the different forms of *balance* in the reading. One meaning of *balance* is "to make things equal."

MATHEMATICS

Strategy Tip

Illustrations in a math text often show how to do a process. What does this illustration show?

NUMBER	DATE	CHECKS ISSUED TO OR DESCRIPTION OF DEPOSIT	(−) AMOUNT OF CHECK	✔ T	(−) CHECK FEE (IF ANY)	(+) AMOUNT OF DEPOSIT	BALANCE
	10/97	TO/FOR Deposit				49.80	49.80
							BAL 49.80
104	11/97	TO/FOR Health Life Magazine	13.50				13.50
							BAL 36.30
105	12/97	TO/FOR Sports Today	40.00				40.00
							BAL -3.70
	12/97	TO/FOR Bounced Check Fee	25.00				25.00
							BAL -28.70
	12/97	TO/FOR Deposit				100.00	100.00
							BAL 71.30

Can you follow the steps to balance this checkbook?

First, review your statement to see whether the bank deducted, or subtracted, any fees from your account. Some banks charge a service fee for operating a checking account. Then review your statement to see whether the bank added any money to your account. Many banks pay interest on the account total. Interest is a type of bonus that is added to your account for having an account at that bank.

Updating Your Total

Once you have deducted your fees and added your interest, you'll want to look over the canceled checks. Compare each check number and amount with your record book. You can make sure you wrote the correct amount of each check in your book. You can also make sure that the bank deducted the correct amount from your account.

Then mark the canceled checks. Most people put check marks next to those entries in their record book. This way, they can quickly see which checks the bank hasn't paid.

Now you are ready to see whether your account balances. Write down the account total listed in your record book. Add any deposits made to the account that are not shown on the statement. From that total, subtract the amount of total checks outstanding. The remainder should equal the amount noted in your record book. That figure is the amount of money you have in your account.

After you finish filling in the L column of your KWL chart, look over your chart. Did you answer all your W questions? Did you find information that would answer questions you didn't ask? Go ahead and make necessary changes to your chart. To make sure you understand how to balance a checkbook, use your chart to write a summary of the selection.

Real-life Math:
Balancing a Checking Account

Apply It. . . . .   To check your understanding of the selection, circle the best answer to each question below.

1. Money put into a bank account is called
   a. a check.
   b. an account.
   c. a deposit.
   d. a statement.

2. The recipient of a check is the
   a. person or company who will receive the money.
   b. date the check was written.
   c. person who has the account.
   d. amount of money in the checking account.

3. Interest is
   a. money the bank deducts from an account.
   b. money the bank adds to an account.
   c. the cost of printing your checks.
   d. a teller who pays attention to your account.

Test Tip

The word *before* shows that question 4 tests your understanding of the steps in a process. To answer this question correctly, you need to identify the first thing you do when balancing your checkbook.

4. When you balance your checkbook, what should you do before you review your canceled checks?
   a. Find the total of outstanding checks.
   b. Check the statement for service fees and interest.
   c. Note the date of the first check written from the account.
   d. Determine the total number of checks you have written.

5. What mathematical operations do you perform when you balance your checkbook?
   a. addition and division
   b. multiplication and subtraction
   c. multiplication and division
   d. addition and subtraction

Use the lines below to write your answers for numbers 6 and 7. Use your KWL chart to help you.

6. Why is it important to balance your checking account?

   _____

   _____

7. List the steps to follow when balancing a checkbook.

   _____

   _____

   _____

Lesson 18

Statistics: Nielsen Ratings

Understand It......

Hint
You can review the DRTA strategy on page 16.

What's your favorite television show? If you ask ten people that question, you'll probably get ten different answers. The answers are very important to the networks that broadcast shows and to the advertisers who buy airtime for their commercials. In this reading, you'll find out why.

Try It..............

Because you probably know enough about TV to make some predictions, the DRTA strategy could be a good choice with this reading. Copy the DRTA chart onto a sheet of paper. Then preview the reading. Make predictions about the kind of information you will learn.

After recording your predictions in the Preview box, read the selection. Gather evidence that backs up your predictions and other important information. Write the evidence in the Take Notes column of the chart. After you read, write a summary of the reading in the Review box.

Strategy Tip
When you preview the selection, look for words that are repeated. *Nielsen Media Research, viewers, meters,* and *ratings* appear often. Focus on these terms as you make your predictions.

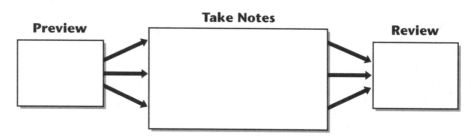

Vocabulary Tip
The word *viewership* might not be familiar, but you probably know the word *viewer*. Reading the paragraph carefully will tell you that *viewership* is another word for *"audience."*

Nielsen Ratings

Your family probably has one thing in common with most American families. The television set is on for some part of every day. In the United States, approximately 99 million households have at least one TV. Each person who watches TV is a possible consumer, or buyer, of a product. Advertisers know that television commercials are one way to reach consumers. They spend almost $40 billion each year on TV ads.

Advertisers want to make sure they spend their money wisely. Therefore, they want to know how many and what kind of people will watch their commercials. So, how do advertisers get that vital information? The Nielsen ratings provide it.

Nielsen Media Research produces the Nielsen ratings. It uses meters to track **viewership**. The company chooses television households at random. If a household agrees to participate, the company places a meter on each TV that notes the program or channel, the time the TV is on, and the number of times the channel changes. The company also collects information about a show's general **audience**. Information about each viewer is collected when he or she presses an identification button.

Statistics:
Nielsen Ratings

In the middle of each night, the company collects information from all the meters. The data is processed, and by noon the following day, networks and advertisers have the ratings. A high Nielsen rating means a large number of households tuned in.

Rating and Market Share

There are two main kinds of information that comprise the Nielsen ratings—the ratings and the share. The *rating* is how many households in the United States were tuned in to a show. Often the rating numbers are followed by the share. The share is the percentage of television sets that are on and tuned to a particular show. Here is how both of these numbers are determined.

The United States has about 99 million households that own TV sets. A 10 rating means that 10 percent of those, or about 9.9 million, were tuned to a show. To determine the rating of a show, you would use this equation:

Strategy Tip
What do these two equations tell you about the Nielsen ratings? Add this information to your DRTA chart.

$$\text{rating} = \frac{\text{households tuned to a show}}{\text{total households with TV sets}} \times 100 \text{ points}$$

The *share* of a show is a comparison between that show and the others on TV at the same time. For example, if a show had a 20 share, 20 percent of the people with their sets on had the sets tuned to that show. Here is how to determine a show's share:

$$\text{share} = \frac{\text{households tuned to a particular show}}{\text{total households with TV sets on}} \times 100 \text{ points}$$

The Cost of Advertising

Once networks have the ratings, they can determine the cost per thousand viewers, or CPM. (*M* is the Roman-numeral sign for "thousands.") Networks look at the ratings to see how popular the show is. They look at the **demographics**, or age, sex, and location of the viewers. The more desirable the demographics are, the more the network can charge for advertising time. For example, younger viewers aged 18 to 24 years old are popular targets for many advertisers. The shows that attract these viewers may have a higher CPM. The CPM for a show might be $4 a minute. If its audience is 2 million viewers, a 60-second commercial would be $8,000. For popular shows, rates can reach $1 million for a minute of commercial time.

Vocabulary Tip
Look around the word *demographics* for context clues that can help you understand its meaning. For example, an author can place a definition between commas.

For special broadcasts like the Superbowl, some advertisers will pay large sums of money. In 1999, the price for a thirty-second commercial during the Superbowl was $1.6 million dollars. At those rates, the CPM is very high. It's the huge number of viewers for such once-a-year events that advertisers are after, and not a reasonable cost per viewer.

The ratings and shares that network television shows earn today are much lower than they were two decades ago. Back then, there were only three networks. If a show had a 30 share, that meant one-third of the people with their TV sets on were watching that show. A 30 share was about average when there were only three choices.

Today, though, there are often 40 or more channels viewers can choose from. If every channel had an equal share, they would each have less than a 3 share. So, in today's TV market, a 30 share is extremely rare. Viewers have many more choices and advertisers have to look at demographics and CPMs more closely.

When you've completed you DRTA chart, look over your notes. Write a few sentences that summarize the main points in the Review section of your chart.

Apply It. . . . . To check your understanding of the selection, circle the best answer to each question below.

1. About how much money do advertisers spend each year on television commercials?
   a. $4 million
   b. $40 million
   c. $40 billion
   d. $400 billion

2. How does Nielsen Media Research gather information about television viewership?
   a. from interviews
   b. through meters
   c. through written surveys sent to television owners
   d. from telephone surveys

3. Nielsen Media Research collects information about all of the following *except*
   a. the number of times the station was changed.
   b. the age of a television viewer.
   c. the number of hours a television set is turned on daily.
   d. the price of a television set.

Test Tip

To find the correct answer to question 4, carefully read each choice. A single word can make an answer wrong or right in a multiple-choice question.

4. The word *share* as used in the section "Rating and Market Share" means
   a. the percentage of people in the United States watching TV.
   b. the percentage of households with TV sets on watching one particular show.
   c. the number of people with TVs who are watching a show.
   d. the number of households who are watching TV.

5. An advertiser would be willing to spend a higher CPM for a show because
   a. it is a show about the product being advertised.
   b. the share is low and the audience is expected to be large.
   c. the show appeals to a demographic the advertiser wants to target.
   d. both a and b

Use the lines below to write your answers for numbers 6 and 7. Use your DRTA chart to help you.

6. List three products that are advertised during TV shows you watch. Describe the audience of the shows.

_____

_____

_____

_____

_____

7. If the CPM for a show is $8 a minute and it has 7 million viewers, how much would a 60-second commercial cost? Describe how you found your answer.

_____

_____

_____

_____

_____

Economics:
Lesson 19 Paying Taxes

Understand It......

Hint

You can review the KWL Plus strategy on page 4.

You are in a store and see something you want to buy. You discover you've got just enough to buy it. However, when the clerk rings up the sale, the total is more than the cost of the item. You forgot about sales tax. In this selection, you will learn about the kinds of taxes people pay.

Use the KWL Plus reading strategy to understand this selection. Even if you don't pay taxes yet or you live in a state that doesn't have a sales tax, you've probably heard people complain about high taxes. When you work, *you* will be a taxpayer.

Try It..............

Copy the KWL chart onto another piece of paper. Then list everything you know about taxes in the K column. In the W column, write what you want to know about the topic. Think about those questions as you read. After you read, write what you've learned in the L column. Then use your KWL chart to write a summary of the selection.

K (What I know)	W (What I want to know)	L (What I've learned)

Strategy Tip

Do you know what happens to the money people pay in taxes? Do you know why workers pay income taxes? You might want to include these questions in the W column of your KWL chart.

Vocabulary Tip

The verb *levy* means "to order to pay." Notice that *charge* follows the word *levy* and tells you its meaning.

Paying Taxes

Taxes are fees that are charged by the government. The government uses tax money to cover the cost of services to the community. Schools are just one of those services. Tax money pays for maintaining roads, operating police and fire departments, running health care facilities, and defending the country.

There are many different kinds of taxes. If you have ever bought an item in a store or eaten a meal in a restaurant, you have probably paid sales tax. Most states **levy**, or charge, a fee on the sale of goods and services. The amount of tax is a certain percentage of the sale. The greater the sale's total, the more tax you pay. For example, if you buy a book that costs $14.00 in a state with 6% sales tax, you would first multiply the price of your book by the percentage that you are being taxed:

$14.00 x .06 = .84. This is your sales tax.

Then, you would add the sales tax to the price of your book.

$14.00 + .84 = $14.84

Therefore, $14.84 is the total price of your book, including the tax.

Workers pay another kind of tax, which is called income tax. In the United States, the federal government and most state governments

Economics:
Paying Taxes

charge workers a percentage of their salaries. A percentage of a worker's wages goes to the federal government, and another percentage goes to the state government. Some city governments also have income taxes.

Most state income taxes are proportional taxes. A proportional tax has a rate that does not change. If the rate is 6%, then every worker pays 6% of his or her income to the state, whether that income is $10,000 or $100,000. To figure out how much state tax you would pay if your income were $50,000, you would multiply your salary by the state tax.

$50,000 x .06 = $3,000.00

If you earned $50,000 a year, $3,000.00 is what you would pay in tax.

Strategy Tip

This income tax form shows you how income tax is figured. Add this information to your KWL chart.

Figure your total income (See page 20.) Attach Copy B of your Forms W-2 and 10099-R here. If you didn't get a W-2, see page 25. Enclose, but do not attach, any payment with your return.	7	Wages, salaries, tips, etc. This should be shown in box 1 of your W-2 form(s). Attach Form(s) W-2			7	
	8a	**Taxable** interest income (see page 25). IF OVER $400, attach Schedule 1.			8a	
	b	**Tax-exempt** interest. DO NOT include on line 8a.		8b		
	9	Dividends. If over $400, attach Schedule 1			9	
	10a	Total IRA distributions 10a		10b	Taxable amount (see page 27)	
	11a	Total pensions and annuities. 11a		11b	Taxable amount (see page 27)	11b
	12	Unemployment compensation (see right page 30).			12	
	13a	Social security benefits. 13a		13b	Taxable amount (see page 31).	13b
	14	Add lines 7 through 13b (far right column). This is your total income			14	
Figure your adjusted gross income	15a	Your IRA deduction (see page 34).		15a		
	b	Spouse's IRA deduction (see page 34).		15b		
	c	Add lines 15a and 15b. These are your **total adjustments**.			15c	
	16	Subtract line 15c from line 14. This is your **adjusted gross income.** If less than $25,296 and a child lived with you (less than $9,000 if a child didn't live with you), see "Earned income credit" on page 44.			16	

A part of a federal income tax form

The income tax levied by the federal government is a progressive tax. The rate of a progressive tax varies. Workers are taxed at different rates, depending on how much money they earn. A worker may pay between 15% and 39.6% of his or her taxable income to the federal government. The higher the income, the more income tax the worker pays.

For example, a worker who earns $20,000 is taxed at a rate of 15%. To figure out how much the worker would pay, multiply the salary of $20,000 by 15%, which would total $3,000.00. That is how much the worker would owe in taxes. A worker who earns $60,000 is taxed at a rate of 31%. That worker would multiply $60,000 by 31%, which would total $18,600. That is the amount of tax the worker would owe.

At the end of each year, employers send information to the IRS by April 15. At that time, people must also pay any income taxes they owe.

Now complete your KWL chart. Be sure to include all the main ideas and enough detail to write a summary of the reading.

Apply It............ To check your understanding of the selection, circle the best answer to each question below.

1. A proportional tax is a tax that
   a. is paid only by wealthy members of a community.
   b. has a rate that does not change.
   c. has a rate that varies.
   d. is paid twice each year.

2. Which of the following statements describes how a worker's income changes the rate of federal income tax?
   a. As income increases, tax rate decreases.
   b. As income increases, tax rate increases.
   c. Tax rate stays the same.
   d. Tax rate varies from state to state.

3. If you buy a hammer that costs $24.00, how much extra would you have to pay if the sales tax is 5%?
   a. $.12
   b. $1.20
   c. $24.12
   d. $25.20

4. Which mathematical operation would you use to figure out the amount of tax a worker will pay if he earns $35,000 and the tax rate is 4%?
   a. $35.00 x .04
   b. $35,000 + .04
   c. $35,000 x .04
   d. $35,000 − .04

5. If a worker earns a salary of $65,000 and the state tax rate is 7%, how much state tax would the worker have to pay?
   a. $4.50
   b. $45
   c. $450
   d. $4,550

Use the lines below to write your answers for numbers 6 and 7. Use your KWL chart to help you.

Test Tip

To answer question 6, you must define both proportional and progressive taxes. You must also tell how they are different.

6. How is a proportional tax different from a progressive tax?

_____

_____

7. Do you think it is fair that federal income tax is a progressive tax? Give reasons for your response.

_____

_____

History:
Lesson 20   Early Mathematics

Understand It......

Hint

You can review the PLAN strategy on page 12.

Math is much more than a subject you study in school. Many of your everyday activities call on your ability to think, solve problems, and communicate using mathematical symbols. People who lived thousands of years ago had similar needs. In this selection, you will discover how those needs led to the development of mathematics.

Try It..............

Try the PLAN strategy to help you focus on the main ideas of the selection. When you use PLAN, you draw a word map that helps you predict what you will read. Copy one of the PLAN word maps below or create your own.

Then predict the kind of information you will read in the article. Record your predictions in your word map. Locate important information you will look for as you read. Write a check mark next to ideas you know about. Write a question mark next to the ideas you don't know about. After you read, add words to your word map that will help you remember this information. Then note what you have learned by reviewing.

Strategy Tip

When you predict what you will read, think of why ancient people may have needed math.

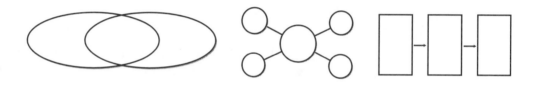

Vocabulary Tip

A definition of *tallies* appears between commas immediately after the word.

Early Mathematics

According to most scientists, the first humans lived in Africa. There, people first developed language, tools, and organized ways of living. People also created mathematics. Mathematics is the use of numbers, shapes, and patterns to describe and explain the world.

In Africa, scientists found evidence of early people's use of math. Archaeologists discovered a fossil bone in a place called Ishango in Zaire. The bone is about 20,000 years old. **Tallies**, or marks that represent number counts, cover the bone.

Some scientists think the Ishango bone was a calendar. Others think it shows that people had discovered how to multiply. They believe the tallies for 3 and 6, 4 and 8, and 5 and 10 show that people knew how to multiply by 2. Although no one knows the specific meaning of the Ishango bone, scientists do know it shows that early humans were thinking mathematically.

Tallies are one way to write numbers. People use tallies to count days or objects. However, using tallies to record numbers presents a problem. It is difficult to write large numbers using tally marks. So people invented a new way to record numbers. Around 3100 B.C., Egyptians in the Nile Valley were using numerals.

The Egyptians still used tallies for numbers 1 through 9. For 10, they used a symbol that stood for 10 tallies. The number 11 was represented by the symbol and one tally mark. The number 12 was represented by the symbol and two tally marks. The Egyptians invented more symbols to write numbers up to 1,000,000. The symbols made representing large numbers much easier. Modern numerals reflect that idea of using symbols instead of tallies.

Strategy Tip

What does this illustration show you about how ancient people used math? Add this information to your PLAN chart.

The Nile Valley dwellers also created a system of measures. They needed a system to figure out fair exchanges in the marketplace. The Egyptians used the length of a forearm to measure cloth. They called that length a cubit. However, problems arose because people's arms are different lengths. A short arm was good for the seller. A long arm was good for the buyer. To make a trade, the buyer and the seller had to agree on the length of the cubit. The Egyptians decided a cubit would be the length of the forearm of the pharaoh or king. That made the cubit a standard length.

The Egyptians made the first calendar that had 365 days in one year.

We can also trace fractions to the ancient Egyptians. To measure fractions of a cubit, they used palms and fingers. Four fingers equaled one palm, and seven palms equaled one cubit. For fine measures, fingers were divided into halves, thirds, fourths, and so on.

The first mathematical ideas were developed without the aid of modern technology. Early Egyptian mathematicians lived thousands of years ago and had few tools to work with. However, their ideas serve as a basis for mathematical ideas used by present-day people.

Now that you have finished reading the selection, complete your PLAN word map. Add notes that explain all the important points. Then review it in your mind or redraw your word map.

History:
Early Mathematics

Apply It . . . . To check your understanding of the selection, circle the best answer to each question below.

1. What does the Ishango bone show?
   a. All Egyptians were farmers.
   b. Early people thought mathematically.
   c. Numbers and shapes are part of math.
   d. Ancient Egyptians could read.

2. What do tallies represent?
   a. number counts
   b. mathematical symbols
   c. different shapes
   d. days of the year

3. Ancient Egyptians used symbols to write numbers up to
   a. 1 billion.
   b. 10 million.
   c. 100 million.
   d. 1 million.

4. How long was a cubit?
   a. the length of the pharaoh's ring finger
   b. the length of a buyer's foot
   c. the length of the queen's palm
   d. the length of the pharaoh's forearm

Test Tip

To correctly answer question 5, think about the title of the selection. A title often provides the reader with clues to the main idea of a selection.

5. What is the main idea of the selection?
   a. People need computers to do math.
   b. Early people made observations of the sky that were used to calculate.
   c. Many mathematical ideas used today were developed by ancient people.
   d. Mathematics has always been an important subject.

Use the lines below to write your answers for numbers 6 and 7. Use your PLAN organizer to help you.

6. List three ways that you use mathematics in your everyday life.

   _____

   _____

   _____

7. Create a system to measure distances around your classroom. List three measures you would use and how they relate to one another.

   _____

   _____

   _____

Lesson 21

Computers: Sharing with Our Neighbors

MATHEMATICS

Understand It.......

Hint
You can review the Cornell Note-taking strategy on page 8.

Do you have a hobby? Do you have a passion for a particular sport? Wouldn't it be great if you could make a career doing something that you really enjoy? In this selection, you will read about a person who turned his passion into a career.

Try It.............

Use the Cornell Note-taking strategy to help you understand the reading. First copy the Cornell Note-taking chart shown below onto another sheet of paper. After you read, you will list the important points and the evidence that supports each point in your Cornell chart. Your notes should focus on the main points, not the minor ones. When you're finished, you can use the chart to write a summary of what you learned.

Strategy Tip
List key words or ideas in the Main Points column. List details that support or explain these key words or ideas in the Evidence/Details column.

Main Points	Evidence/Details

Strategy Tip
Previewing the topic sentences will show you that this selection is a biography. As you read, look for information about why Granderson is important. Add these facts to your Cornell notes.

Sharing with Our Neighbors

Kenneth A. Granderson has always liked to explore new ideas. When his high school got its first computer, Granderson gave it a try. "With computers, I found I could explore almost anything," he says. Granderson later turned his passion for computers into a career.

Granderson creates computer software, the programs that people use with their computers. His company is called ICS (Inner City Software). The name hints at more than the company's location. It is a clue to Granderson's greatest mission.

Finding the Perfect Fit

Kenneth Granderson grew up in a poor section of Brooklyn, New York. He worked hard in high school. On Saturdays and during summers, he attended computer classes for teens held at a local college. Granderson's hard work earned him entrance to MIT (Massachusetts Institute of Technology) in Boston, Massachusetts. He majored in electrical engineering.

Granderson's studies at MIT "taught me how to tackle big and complex problems," he says. "You need this skill to develop software."

Computers:
Sharing with Our Neighbors

Granderson graduated from MIT in 1985. He went to work for a large company, testing software made by other people. Then he began to write his own programs. He started ICS in 1992.

A Universe of Possibilities

ICS is based in Dorchester, Massachusetts. Dorchester is a section of Boston where many African Americans and people from other minority groups live. Most Dorchester families have little money. ICS has clients all over the world, but the people Granderson really wants to reach are right in his neighborhood.

Granderson urges people who live in poorer areas of cities to use computers. He believes technology can improve the lives of poorer people. Computers can link people to the world outside their neighborhoods. They offer **access** to an endless flow of ideas and information. Technology "can open up a universe of possibilities," Granderson says.

If people who live in poorer areas can benefit from these possibilities, what keeps kids in big cities from using computers? Granderson thinks one problem is a lack of programs that appeal to city kids. He is trying to change that. He plans to develop as much software geared to big-city teenagers as he can. His first project was about the history of African Americans in Boston. He also led a major Internet project. The Internet is a network that links computers around the world. It allows the people in Dorchester to "share our creative output with our neighbors and the world."

Kenneth Granderson

The number of people who use computers grows every day. Kenneth Granderson wants kids to be part of that trend. He wants kids to look beyond their neighborhoods and use computers to see what the world might have to offer them.

When you finish reading, create your Cornell chart. Then use your chart to write a summary of the selection. Your summary should include the important points of Granderson's life and details to support them.

Vocabulary Tip

The word *access* means "a way or means of entering."

Apply It. . . . . To check your understanding of the selection, circle the best answer to each question below.

1. Software is
   a. a new type of computer.
   b. a course that teaches teens how to use computers.
   c. college classes in electrical engineering.
   d. programs used with computers.

2. What is Granderson's "greatest mission"?
   a. to become president of a large company
   b. to show others how technology can improve their lives
   c. to design the world's fastest computer
   d. to expand the Internet

3. Granderson wants big-city kids to learn how to use the Internet
   a. so they can find well-paying jobs.
   b. so they can research school reports.
   c. so that they can share their knowledge with the world.
   d. so they can develop their math skills.

4. The author wrote the selection to
   a. inform.
   b. entertain.
   c. persuade.
   d. express an opinion.

Test Tip

A conclusion is a judgment or decision reached after careful thought. To answer question 5, think about what you learned about Kenneth Granderson in this selection.

5. What can you conclude about Kenneth Granderson?
   a. He enjoys living in the Northeast.
   b. He is a hard-working, determined person.
   c. He insists on being in charge of a project.
   d. He would like to become a teacher.

Use the lines below to write your answers for numbers 6 and 7. Use your Cornell notes and summary to help you.

6. What can young people learn by reading about Kenneth A. Granderson?

_____

_____

7. Write a paragraph explaining how computers have affected your everyday life.

_____

_____

_____

_____

Problem Solving:
Lesson 22 Mental Math

Understand It......

Hint
You can review the DRTA strategy on page 16.

You make mathematical calculations in your head every day. You look at your change and decide if you have enough to buy a soda. You estimate what the tip on a meal will be. In this selection, you will learn to make different kinds of calculations in your head.

Try It..............

DRTA is a good reading strategy to use with this selection because you probably know something about mental math. Copy the DRTA chart below onto a sheet of paper. Then preview the reading. Write predictions in the chart about the kind of information it contains.

After recording your predictions in the chart, read the selection. Look for information that supports your predictions. Write this information in the Take Notes column. Then summarize the selection in the Review column.

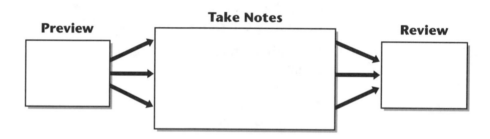

Preview   Take Notes   Review

Mental Math

Figuring out problems in your head, or using mental math, is a very handy skill. How often have you used a piece of paper and a pencil to figure out the answer to a problem? With some new methods, you will be able to use mental math.

Vocabulary Tip
The word *round* has a meaning in math that is different from its meaning in other subjects. When you round a number in math, you make a number larger or smaller so you can work with it more easily.

Working with Round Numbers

When you **round** a number, you go up or down to a number that is easier to use. Let's say you wanted to add 497 and 354. Those numbers look difficult to add in your head, but the operation becomes easier when you round them. Here's how to do it:

Step 1: Round the numbers, remembering what you added or subtracted. For example, rewrite the numbers above:

497 = (500–3)

354 = (350+4)

When you are reading math that contains steps or an equation, review by creating a problem and then solving it. That will show if you understand the process.

Step 2: Add the rounded numbers.

```
 500
+350
 850
```

Step 3: To find the exact answer, add or subtract the numbers left over after rounding.

```
4–3 = 1
 850        497
+   1      +354
 851        851
```

The same technique works for subtraction, as well. You subtract your rounded numbers, and then add or subtract the leftover numbers.

Adding by Place Value

In math textbooks, you will often see terms explained with both a definition and examples. What does *place value* mean?

If you need to add or subtract larger numbers, you can add or subtract by working with **place value**—ones, tens, hundreds, and so on. For example, imagine you have to add 526 and 493. Here's how you can break down those numbers.

Step 1: Add the largest place value, or the hundreds, together.

```
 500
+400
 900
```

Step 2: Add the next largest place value. In this case, add the tens together.

```
 20
+90
110
```

Step 3: Add the next largest grouping. In this case, add the ones.

```
 6
+3
 9
```

Step 4: Add the numbers from each operation for the total.

```
  900
  110
+   9
1,019 Total
```

Problem Solving:
Mental Math

Multiplying the Pieces

When you multiply large numbers, you can break the numbers into smaller figures that are easier to work with. Follow these steps.

Step 1: Suppose you are multiplying 23 X 17. First, make one number smaller so you can multiply in your head. In this case, you would break 23 into 20 X 3.

Step 2: Now, multiply the second number by each of the numbers you broke down.

Multiply 20 by 17   17 X 20 = 340

Multiply 3 by 17   3 X 17 = 51

Step 3: To get the final answer, add those two numbers. Check your answer by multiplying the original numbers.

```
340        Check:    23
+51                 ×17
391                 161
                    +23
                    391
```

Try these techniques next time you need to do math in your head. Remember that you can use these methods with money, units, or any kinds of numbers.

Look over your DRTA notes. Did you include all the important parts you learned about mental math? Write a few sentences that summarize the selection in the Review box of your chart.

Apply It. . . . . To check your understanding of the selection, circle the best answer to each question below.

Test Tip

Question 1 tests your ability to sequence the steps in a process. The words *immediately before* show that you must name the last thing to do before you add the extra numbers.

1. When you add by rounding numbers, what should you do after you rewrite the numbers?
   a. Add the rounded numbers.
   b. Subtract the rounded numbers.
   c. Round the numbers.
   d. Read the problem.

2. If you are adding 289 to 876 by using place value, what would you do first?
   a. Set up an equation.
   b. Subtract 200 from 800.
   c. Add 80 to 70.
   d. Add 200 and 800.

3. "If you need to add or subtract larger numbers, you can add or subtract by working with place value, or the parts of the numbers—ones, tens, hundreds, and so on." In that sentence, *place value* means
   a. whether the numbers are 100s, 10s, or 1s.
   b. larger or smaller than 10.
   c. equal to another number.
   d. none of the above

4. What do these mental math calculations have in common?
   a. They all deal with subtraction and addition.
   b. They all deal with addition and multiplication.
   c. They all work with numbers that are easier to use.
   d. They all need a calculator.

5. What is the main idea of this selection?
   a. You can solve any simple equation with pencil and paper.
   b. Following a plan can only help you answer problems that have large numbers.
   c. You can solve math problems without pencil and paper.
   d. The same plan can be used to solve any kind of math problem.

Use the lines below to write your answers for numbers 6 and 7. Use your DRTA chart to help you.

6. Describe a situation in which you would use one of these mental math methods.

   _____

   _____

   _____

7. Write an explanation for how you would multiply 35 by 18 using mental math.

   _____

   _____

   _____

Unit 5 Review
Reading in Mathematics

In this unit, you have practiced using the KWL Plus, Cornell Note-taking, PLAN, and DRTA strategies. Choose one strategy and use it when you read the selection below. Use a separate sheet of paper to draw charts, take notes, and summarize what you learn.

Hint | *Remember that all reading strategies have activities for before, during, and after reading. To review these steps, look back at Unit 1 or the last page of this book.*

The Line on Geometry

From the time of the ancient Egyptians and Babylonians, people have used geometry. In ancient times, geometry was mainly concerned with very basic information. People wanted to find ways to create straight angles so buildings would be straight.

The 6th-century Greek mathematician Pythagoras was the father of scientific geometry. Pythagoras was born on the island of Samos, but he left because of his dislike for the tyrannical leader Polycrates. About 550 B.C., he settled in southern Italy. The movement he founded there was based on his religious, political, and philosophical beliefs. Today, everything that we know about Pythagoras comes from his followers.

Pythagoras and his group made major contributions to the study of mathematics and geometry. One of his most famous contributions is the equation $a^2+b^2=c^2$. This equation is called the Pythagoreon Theorem, which states that the square of the hypotenuse of a right triangle is equal to the sum of the squares of the other two sides.

Other Greeks contributed to the study of geometry too. Perhaps the most famous geometry textbook ever written is Euclid's *Elements*. Despite his lack of sophisticated knowledge or techniques, Euclid was able to create a textbook for geometry that served as the basis for the study of geometry up to the present day.

From the time of the ancient Greeks to the end of the Middle Ages, there was little groundbreaking work done in geometry. Then, in the 16th century, the French thinker René Descartes published his important work *A Discourse on Method*. Descartes was able to show the relationship between geometry and algebra. He showed how the methods used in algebra could be used by geometry, and vice versa. This work is the basis of analytic geometry, which in turn is the basis for much of the work in geometry today.

In analytic geometry, the figures of geometry—lines, curves, shapes—can be represented by a table of halves or an algebraic equation, and a graph in a coordinate system. A student can locate a point in three-dimensional space with a set of coordinates.

Descartes's breakthrough of using numbers to describe geometric positions was also responsible in part for advanced work in calculus and other fields in higher mathematics.

Another branch of geometry, descriptive geometry, is the basis for much work in engineering and architecture today. To do their jobs, architects and engineers often must rely on making accurate two- and three-dimensional models that demonstrate the relationship of these forms in space.

Use your notes and charts to help you answer the questions below.

1. Euclid's *Elements* is notable because
   a. it was the first geometry textbook used by the Greeks.
   b. it was used as a textbook for geometry.
   c. it went against the established wisdom of the time.
   d. it was the basis for the Pythagorean Theorem.

2. René Descartes was important to the field of geometry because
   a. he linked geometry and algebra.
   b. his textbook is still used today.
   c. he invented descriptive geometry.
   d. both b and c

3. Architects and engineers use descriptive geometry because
   a. it allows them to represent three-dimensional models accurately.
   b. it is useful when designing buildings.
   c. it is the basis of geometry.
   d. both a and b

4. Explain the importance of Pythagoras to the field of geometry.

   _____

   _____

5. Describe some of the uses of geometry today.

   _____

   _____

Vocabulary Handbook

No one knows every word. Because of this, you need to know how to learn unfamiliar words. You may immediately look up a word you do not know. Someone else may look for how a word is used in a sentence. In this Vocabulary Handbook, you will learn some new methods for figuring out the meaning of words you do not know. You may also review methods you already use.

Using Word Maps to Understand Unknown Words

Sometimes you must understand one word to understand an entire chapter or article. You may know right away that you need to understand a word—when, for example, it is in the title of the reading.

Perhaps you are reading a textbook chapter that is titled "How Photosynthesis Works." If you do not know what *photosynthesis* means, you need to find out to understand the reading. Preview the selection to collect information about the word. Here is a word map about the word *photosynthesis*:

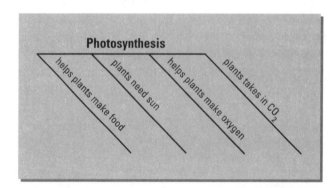

The reader who made this word map now has some ideas about what photosynthesis is. He or she knows that it helps plants make food, that plants need sun to complete it, that it helps plants make oxygen, and that plants take in carbon dioxide when they are photosynthesizing. Now the reader can better understand the selection.

In these lessons, you will learn more ways to help you figure out the meaning of the words you read.

Exercise 1   Context Clues: Part I

Understand It...... Active readers use context clues to figure out the meaning of words they do not know. Context clues can help you understand what words mean.

- **Look at the words around the one you do not know.** When you find clues from context, you examine words around the one you do not know. These words will often give you hints about the meaning of the new word.

- **Look for all the times the word is used.** Sometimes a word you don't know is repeated or restated. Look at the places the word is used for clues.

Read this paragraph and use context clues to understand the words in bold type.

> An iceberg is an **immense** piece of ice that floats in the ocean. **Berg** is the German word for mountain. So an iceberg is a mountain of ice. Icebergs are dangerous because they are so immense, or big. Only a very small part of an iceberg is **visible**, though. The rest of the iceberg is hidden beneath the surface of the water.

Try It.............. To check your understanding of the vocabulary words, circle the best answer to each question below.

1. *Immense* means
   a. beneath the surface.
   b. "mountain" in German.
   c. dangerous.
   d. very big.

2. Which context clues did you use to define *immense?*

   _____

   _____

3. "Only a very small part of an iceberg is visible, though. The rest of the iceberg is hidden beneath the surface of the water." In this sentence, *visible* means
   a. able to be seen.
   b. hidden.
   c. dangerous.
   d. big.

4. Which context clues did you use to define *visible?*

   _____

   _____

Exercise 2 Context Clues: Part II

Understand It...... Sometimes writers make it easy for readers to understand difficult words. They add definitions, restatements, or synonyms. At other times, writers use examples that show the word's meaning, or they compare or contrast the word to other known words. Once you know these tools, you will understand more of what you read. Here are some of those tools.

- **Definitions, restatements, and synonyms.** Authors often help readers by defining a word when it is used. They may also restate the meaning of the word or show the meaning through a synonym. Here are some examples:

  Definition: She studied **geology,** which is the study of the earth.

  Restatement: The **proprietor,** or the owner, of the restaurant came out to greet us.

  Synonym: Frieda felt so **isolated,** so alone that she didn't even want to go to the party.

- **Meaning through example.** Sometimes authors use an example to show the meaning of a word. They may signal that they are giving an example by words such as *for instance, for example,* and *such as.* Here is an example:

  The student center provides many **resources,** such as tutoring, workshops, and a library full of helpful booklets.

- **Comparisons and contrasts.** A sentence may include a comparison that shows how one word is like another word. The words *like, as,* and *similar to* may signal this. A contrast shows how a word is unlike another word. Look for signals such as *but, however, on the contrary,* and *on the other hand.* Here are some examples:

  Comparison: Carley was **skeptical** about her study partner, but stopped questioning his ability once they both passed the test.

  Contrast: Maddie was **famished,** but even her great hunger wouldn't let her start eating before everyone was seated at the table.

Try It. . . . . Use context tools to help you understand the meaning of the words in bold type. Then answer the questions.

> Scientists often do experiments. An experiment is something that is done to find out why things happen. Experiments are used to test a **hypothesis,** or educated guess.
>
> Most experiments in biology are **controlled experiments**. In a controlled experiment, two set-ups are used. Everything about the two set-ups is exactly the same. One set-up, the control, is left alone. In the other set-up, one thing, called the **variable,** is changed. Both experiments are then observed. Any differences in the results of the two set-ups will be due to the one thing that was changed.

To check your understanding of the vocabulary entries, circle the best answer to each question below.

1. A *hypothesis* is
    a. an educated guess.
    b. an experiment.
    c. a laboratory.
    d. both a and b

2. Which context clues helped you choose an answer to question 1?

    _____

3. Which is the best definition for the word *variable?*
    a. a hypothesis
    b. one thing in an experiment that is not changed
    c. one thing in an experiment that is changed
    d. an experiment

4. Which context clues helped you choose an answer to question 3?

    _____

5. If you perform a *controlled experiment,*
    a. you use two set-ups.
    b. you leave one set-up alone and change one thing in the other set-up.
    c. you don't pay attention to the differences in the results once the experiment is over.
    d. both a and b

6. Which context clues helped you choose an answer to question 5?

    _____

    _____

Exercise 3 Prefixes and Suffixes

Understand It...... Prefixes are the parts of words that are added to the beginnings of root words to make new words. Suffixes are the parts of words that are added to the end of root words to make new words. These add-ons change the meaning of a word. You may already know more of these than you think.

Example	Prefixes	Root Word	Suffix
meaningless	—	meaning	-less (without)

Meaning: Without meaning.

Example	Prefixes	Root Word	Suffix
preview	pre- (before or ahead of time)	view	—

Meaning: To view before or ahead of time.

Example	Prefixes	Root Word	Suffix
disrespectful	dis- (not, away from, or opposite of)	respect	-full (full of)

Meaning: Not showing any respect.

Example	Prefixes	Root Word	Suffix
rechargeable	re- (again)	charge	-able (able to be)

Meaning: Able to be charged again.

Example	Prefixes	Root Word	Suffix
unpleasantness	un- (not)	pleasant	-ness (the state or condition of)

Meaning: The state of not being pleasant.

Try It.............. Read the sentences below. Decide on the meaning of the words by looking at the prefixes and suffixes attached to the root words.

1. The root word in *redesign* is: _____

2. *Redesign* means _____

3. The root word in *thankful* is: _____

4. *Thankful* means _____

5. The root word in *uncomfortable* is: _____

6. *Uncomfortable* means _____

Exercise 4   Words with Multiple Meanings

Understand It...... A word may appear in different subject areas and have a different meaning in each one. Here are two ways to help you understand the meaning of words with multiple meanings.

1. Choose from among the meanings you know. You may know that the word *school* can mean two things. A *school* can be a place for learning. A *school* also can be a large number of fish traveling in a group. When you see a word that you know has more than one meaning, think about what you are reading. Which meaning would fit better?

2. Pause if the word you know doesn't make sense. For example, you may know one meaning of the word *pupil*. A *pupil* can be the dark opening in the center of the eye. But read this sentence:

> Celia was the best **pupil** in the class.

The meaning in that sentence is different from the one you may know. If you find a word you think you know, but that word doesn't make sense, look it up. That word probably has multiple meanings.

Below are two passages that use the same words in different ways. Read both passages. Then look at the words in bold type. Use the suggestions above to understand what the words mean in each passage. Then answer the questions.

> **Example 1** I had been watching for days because this is what I decided to do my science report on. Suddenly, it appeared as if out of nowhere. The **cardinal** flew into our **yard.** The beautiful red bird quickly found a place on a branch. Luckily, our **yard** is full of trees, so the **cardinal** was happy to stay long enough for me to observe him.
>
> **Example 2** "The **cardinal**, or number one, rule," said our new teacher, "is that every math student must learn the basic units of measurement." That day, we learned that a **yard** is equal to 3 feet.

Try It............... To check your understanding of the vocabulary words, circle the best answer to each question below.

1. In the first example, the word *cardinal* means
   a. a swaying branch.
   b. a red bird.
   c. a cool breeze.
   d. both a and b

2. Which of these is the best definition for *yard* in Example 2?
   a. 3 feet
   b. a form of measurement
   c. a grassy stretch of land
   d. both a and b

3. Which of the following statements is *false*?
   a. In the first example, *cardinal* is another word for "bird."
   b. The meaning of *yard* is the same in both examples.
   c. In Example 2, *cardinal* means "important."
   d. In Example 1, *yard* means "a grassy stretch of land."

More words with multiple meanings: Sometimes a word that we use every day has a different meaning in a particular content area. Read the two definitions for each word below. Then choose a word from the list that goes with both definitions. Write the word on the line.

host	bank	value	scale	motion

4. _____
   Common use: a place where money is deposited
   Geography: land along the edge of a river

5. _____
   Common use: a weighing machine
   Science: a small, flat plate that forms the covering for fishes

6. _____
   Common use: a movement from one place to another
   Social Studies: an official recommendation made in a meeting

7. _____
   Common use: a fair or proper exchange; what something is worth
   Math: the amount that a symbol stands for

8. _____
   Common use: a person who entertains guests at his or her own expense
   Science: any organism on or in which another lives

Exercise 5   Direction Words

Understand It. . . . . . There are some words you need to know to succeed in school. They are words that are often used in textbooks and on tests. Once you understand these direction words, you will better understand test questions.

Below is a list of common words and their meanings. You will see these words in textbooks and test questions.

> **Describe**—create a picture with words
>
> **Explain**—give facts or reasons for something; give directions
>
> **List**—give examples
>
> **Compare**—show how things are the same
>
> **Contrast**—show how things are different
>
> **Illustrate**—give examples
>
> **Summarize**—write a brief answer stating the important points
>
> **Discuss**—present ideas about a topic
>
> **Analyze**—explain how things are related to one another
>
> **Identify**—place a person or event in time
>
> **Define**—give the meaning of

Try It. . . . . To check your understanding of the direction words, circle the best answer to each question below.

1. The word *analyze* means
    a. to create a vivid picture of the story.
    b. to show differences.
    c. to write a brief answer stating the important points.
    d. to explain how things are related.

2. When you *compare* two books, you should
    a. write how they are the same.
    b. write how they are the same and how they are different.
    c. describe both books.
    d. write how the books are different.

3. When you *define* a vocabulary word, you
    a. give facts about the word.
    b. give its meaning.
    c. explain how it is related to other words.
    d. show how it is different from other words.

First circle the direction word in each of the following questions. Then write your answers on the lines.

4. Summarize your favorite story.

_____

_____

_____

_____

_____

5. List five movies.

_____

_____

_____

_____

_____

6. Describe your best friend.

_____

_____

_____

_____

_____